Lake Effect

Volume 27 / Spring 2023

Penn State Erie / The Behrend College
ISSN 1538-3105
www.behrend.psu.edu/lakeeffect

Contents

Fiction

Poetry

Aimee Parkison

Kindness Among the Looted Bodies

The hawk as it returns to its nest, mushrooms growing in fallen leaves, trees along the lakeshore, songs of every last moment echoed, you turning sixteen and dressing your dog like a lion in the golden leaves of autumn.

Among children biking through neighborhood streets, you were lost. Men rode horses into fields to find you the autumn you disappeared to fall in what I dreamed was love.

You fell in love with the fiddle player who spoke to you through music.

In Louisiana, his ballads, ever changing as a sky before a storm, swept you into two-steps with his friends and brothers, his sisters who became your sisters, knowing the ways of folk musicians. In songs they loved each other. Their songs became a part of you, a name woven into echoes along the water after floods.

Rain changes everything in the golden light of old mansions where people aren't supposed to go unless they are invited to cook, clean, or sing for the rich. Even as a child, you understood why people like us, who had no money, danced in rain.

At night, you are lost. I dream you dancing.

I dream you falling into the fiddler's welcoming arms.

I dream you into his music as rain falls over forests of melody.

Lyrics in his eyes, the rivers and the railyards, the paddle wheel inside you complaining about the men always asking him to play Black Betty because his sisters are tired of singing, tired of you asking why the whip in southern prisons used to torture men is a woman.

Amazing Grace was also a woman, his mother's name, Grace, the thing that will save us from ourselves as we worry for you, attempting to understand if lost means forever.

When we found the opossum stranded in a tree after the flood, the land had become water. The fiddle player paddled his boat to the opossum and climbed the tree to help the opossum down only for you to watch in silence, then in cheering, as the opossum scrambled away from him and back up the tree.

Some stranded people are like the opossum in the tree. They don't want to be saved, even when their world is gone; they don't want a stranger coming to grab them from their last anchor. They hold. But some are like me, waiting for the stranger. I never knew until he sang a song about a woman who walked into the water to enter her flooded house, to find the rooms where her husband and child had drowned to be with them again. Glimpsing her face reflected in the water, the woman swam the flooded streets, knowing she could never go back.

If all bodies are looted by death, some of us have our bodies looted when we are still alive. I spent days and nights searching for you before spending years searching for your body.

The fiddler's sisters sing about a funeral home where a lonely undertaker lovingly caresses the bodies of dead women. The necrophiliac could never caress the living, and I wonder why, why is it so hard for people to see each other and know each other when they are needing each other, why a living woman creates fear and revulsion in some men thrilled by the bodies of the dead.

I try not to think of our mother's friend in college, the one our family keeps thinking of when they are terrified of what happened to you, imagining the girl who was beaten with a wooden log by a stranger who wanted to separate her from her body. He had no use for her body while she was still inside of it where she could see him with her eyes. A neighbor found her body, headless, because her killer had kept her head to wash and style her hair and put makeup on her face as if she were a doll. He killed her so he could have her head, which meant nothing to him until it was taken from her.

Because she's more than a headless woman, more than a looted body, you ask the fiddler to play a song for her. He asks her name, what she was like, where she lived, what she dreamed. He asks nothing about her head or her body or her murderer, and that's one of the reasons you fall for the fiddler. You feel her spirit soaring in his song.

Aimee Parkison

Murder Ballads

Sometimes his songs flowed like the river, cutting through the forest, and sometimes you could enter the songs like the rooms of familiar houses where you lived long ago. Falling in love with the fiddle player meant strange houses became familiar in song, though you never ventured inside until he fiddled the doors open.

Just by playing the fiddle, he told you what he wanted more than he could say with words. He played for hours, which took strength and skill. He played until sweat ran down his long-wet hair on the tavern stage as if he had been drenched in rain.

Later, you would lick the sweat off his eyelids, knowing how jealous women and girls would become since he could kiss you by playing his fiddle. He could work you over without touching your body, stroking you with sound. You often wondered if it were a game he played, then you realized this was no game. He was doing it to other women.

Sometimes when he sang songs, he sang the dead alive so you knew them better than you knew the living, his sisters singing along, gazing into your eyes until you wanted to be a singer, to be some sort of musician so you could be part of their world where the dead breathed through song.

You became the rattler. The girls gave you a rattle so you could shake it, twitching into garden. Going into song with your rattle was the most exciting thing you ever did, stepping on stage with them at the barn dances like trespassing until you realized you were part of the band, dancing.

The dead danced shadows for him and for you and for the music he wanted to haunt. To join them on the road at night, as the van drove the highway, you stroked his long chestnut hair, fingers strumming his beard as he slept.

Careful, careful now, his sisters whispered with their eyes as night became morning. He needs to sleep through dawn since he works the stage into tavern light.

This is the moment you realize he trusts you enough to fall asleep in your arms and has given you the gift of loving you enough to let you cradle him even as he sleeps, to trust you to hold him sleeping as you watch his eyes darting beneath his lids while wondering if he dreams of you.

One night when he's sleeping with his head resting on your lap, his older sister tells you their mother was strangled by their father in a drunken rage. Never speak of her because they saw her die, the other sisters warn, though they speak of her at night while he sleeps until you make the mistake of reminding the older sister what was said and she claims you are mistaken. This moment becomes another forgotten memory because his murder ballads are love songs where the mother is unwritten, her face gazing through the van's dark windows.

David Shumate

Beneath the Full Moon

As the moon ripens from crescent to plump, my dreams turn to carnivals. The gentlest people become brutal. Buddha arm wrestles his followers. Jesus teaches his disciples the seven deadly karate moves. My great-grandmother waves a sword as she leads a band of rioters down the avenue. Bears lumber down the alleys searching for widows to make into mates. The man who lives in the boughs of our maple tree leans down and complains that no one has fed him for weeks. Even you, known for your unfaltering kindness, sported a pair of horns last night at a debutante ball. Three more days until the moon is full. I eat persimmons. I drink mushroom tea. I read books and catch up on correspondence. I would go fishing if the river weren't frozen. I would call you up, but only in dreams do the dead answer their telephones.

David Shumate

On Normal Days

It is difficult to know if this will be a normal day. Various factors must be taken into account. The posture of the moon. The placement of the planets. The banker flicking on his light at the appointed hour can be misleading. So, too, the milkman's bottles rattling. The gardener's dog barking in the half light. The town Casanova starting his car behind his latest lover's bungalow. The unexpected insinuates itself in the smallest crevice it can find. The preacher's wife shows up at the grocery store in an orange hat and winks at the stocking clerk as he places her onions in a bag. A peacock appears in a parking lot and fans out his tail in front of a nun. The man who spent seven months in a coma clears his throat and as the nurse leans down, he whispers *Artichoke*. The weatherman pauses in his forecast, sets down his pointer and stares into the camera to confess to his viewers that ever since he was a child he's been afraid of the rain.

David Shumate

Chinese Painting

In the northern Sung style of painting, Chinese artists depict men and women in mountain retreats made miniscule by the forests surrounding them. Sometimes you have to scan those landscapes to find the human figures tucked away on a pagoda or crossing an arching bridge or traveling through a valley on the back of a mule. The features of their faces are seldom clear. And if you look long enough, the ink lines of the silk painting play a trick and you become the one seated in the pagoda sipping sweet tea. You hear someone ambling down the mountain path. A friend from the next valley bringing vegetables in his basket. Or the woman who sells herbs that drive evil away. Or a lover in a thin gown returned from bathing in a cool stream. A cuckoo calls in the distance. Its mate replies. The museum guard's fingers feel like rainwater dripping from the eaves of that mountain hermitage as he taps you on the shoulder.

Mark Sullivan

Chalk Drawing

Spending the morning trying to find a rhythm, a mood,
I think of the way visual artists can use
observational drawing to spark some connection or
theme, and then try to remember who said, *To draw
a line is to have an idea.* Whoever it was, she or
he meant something about the way the undivided
page becomes active, almost alert, the moment a mark
establishes some shorthand for space, registers
as conscious intention. The way a field, overgrown with
wild grasses and flowers in midsummer, shimmers
into an environment as a doe and her fawn ease
through it from the dark of bordering trees. Or as when
you touch someone and the place of contact belongs
to neither of you but makes an opening where
the electrons of your nerve endings stage a free-form dance.
Lately, when I run in the park, I see the children,
masked and released from classrooms for an indefinite
future, making drawings in chalk on the walkways
and the verges of the closed through road. Schematic faces
and flowers, rainbows and ponies, hearts with tender

endearments written inside, all in the pale blues
        and yellows
    and pinks of crushed calcium mixed with some binder
and pigment, then molded into these soft cylinders
    of color, perfect for small hands. Erratic
        and overlapping,
the images seem to emerge from pre-history, a technology
    of edges and angles, the shapes bending with
        the contours
of rock. In the caves, figures separated by thousands
    of years, horses or lions, leap across each other
as though contained in the same eyeblink. The impulse
    to record and to mark one's presence as enduring
and as transient as graffiti. We used to marvel, in
        the Village,
    at the sidewalk artists who would set out a hat
        for change
or singles and transfer a familiar masterpiece from
        its museum
    walls or church fresco onto the pavements along
        Sixth Avenue.
The Delphic Sibyl and her astonished eyes casting
    a nervous teenager's look at being removed from
        the Sistine
ceiling and chalked virtuosically under our feet. Over days,
    she would be rubbed back into blankness by the river
of thousands of journeys and errands, by the indifference
    of weather. Last week, when I finally ventured
beyond the neighborhood, those same streets
        were teeming

with emptiness, plywood sealing the storefronts, as if
time had stopped its forward motion and was caught
between frames. The collective life we had
been leading—
the life of pizza slices eaten while walking, of parking
tickets festooning the windshields of abandoned cars,
of chess matches in the parks and jazz quartets
in the tunnels—had vanished, and in its place the tawdry
depredations of light rummaged through the remains.
You wondered would that life ever return or was it
the blink
between the arcing strokes on the dark wall, the millennia
dissolving between galloping bodies. *To draw a line . . .*
but for that you need tool and surface, burnt cinder
or compressed lead, plastered vault or gum-blotched
cement. Need the meeting of hand in its extended
and more lasting reach—the electricity coursing through
the cable—with the world's openness and resistance.
So that in the texture made by the bumps
and depressions,
the minute particles of remaining will adhere. So that
the cartoon
barbell will bend into a rainbow with, beneath it,
the caption *Stay Strong*. So that, in this residue, the aurochs
will rear, and the ponies will prance for a time,
in time. The prophetess will raise her girlish glance again
where we walk, and once again we step over and fail to
look down.

Jessica Cuello

Love, Untethered

No love is benign, writes Etel Adnan.

When I was five I made a Mother's Day card from a folded piece of construction paper. The edges did not meet. I used every crayon to draw the rainbow arcs, even the broken pieces. No empty space, no white between them. Black, moon red, aquamarine, magenta, gold. I pressed the wax so hard little flecks clung to the paper. It smelled like resin, like my brother's ear, like the valve of a school instrument passed from child to child, like the meaty, human odor in the hallway where a sick person has been forgotten.

My mother called me to the living room, something she did when I was in trouble, which was often. On the far corner of the table, the card burned in its offense, crinkled without being touched, glinted with the flat gleam of glass eyes like the ones on my doll that I tapped at night, and once kissed, then said *sorry sorry* because she moved from my lips, from the pain of my touch. I heard her hum. My mother gestured to the card as evidence. Inside it said, *I love you even when you're mean.* The coffee table was a barricade. Even when she hit, a spoon kept distance. Our only closeness was when we crossed the street, her tight hold, her clenched mouth.

How do you think that makes me feel? She asked about the card. She meant my expression of true love. *You should not be crying,* she said, *I should be the one crying.* I took the card back to get it right. I failed at gifts again and again. The tea thrown out. The book too sad. The words too strange. The love wrong, wrapped in string. I learned hurt's hum, its fragile notes and edicts, learned that it sang out from a sore and I could wound it without touching—without even trying.

No love is static. Not even the love we can't touch or hold: one-sided love. Isn't that God?

Somewhere we were taught that love moves back and forth between people. A giving and taking. I felt more pain from the love I could not give than the love I could not get. I felt great shame that my love was repulsed. Yet it did not disappear. Instead, it transformed into a strange energy I carried with me. I was aware of this longing and what form it might take.

When my daughter was three I remember watching her eat an ear of corn. I felt overwhelming love for her, for the act itself, an animal love that took over my chest. Her devouring of the corn, the turning of the cob in her chubby fingers, the sound of her teeth breaking the skin, was my own love in its visible form. It left my body and moved freely in a way that I had always desired.

In her essay "The Cost for Love We Are Not Willing to Pay," Etel Adnan describes an early childhood memory where her mother takes her to the sea: *My mother would sit on one of these rocks and let me paddle in the water. As a measure of security, she passed under my arms a string or cord, something like a leash tha she held carefully. Thus I developed from my early years a sensuous response to the sea, a fascination, a need that I lived like a secret. It enchanted me, and it isolated me. It has lasted all my life.*

Love is deeply connected to teaching in my mind, to the act of showing another person what something is. Even more, love is connected to presence. It is the opposite of invisibility.

When I was six my mother took me by hand to a solitary protest. She had spent ten dollars on a toaster that didn't work. It was the 70s. We were poor. $10 was a lot of money. When she went to return the toaster they refused to take it back. We walked back—she had no car—and stood outside the store at the only strip mall in our small town. She lifted her sign: **This store sells broken toasters.** The store relented quickly and we walked home an hour later, a new toaster cradled in her arms.

This lesson of the toaster eluded me, even though I witnessed the entire thing. I did not learn to stand up for myself from it. Instead, I learned to guard against return like I was the toaster.

My presence hurt her. Though she held my hand when we crossed the street, I was not present to her. She was responsible for me, and yet, I knew I was noxious to her. It took me a long time to admit that, it felt so shameful. I am afraid to write it down in this paragraph. How embarrassing to admit that your mother finds you repulsive. Since my absent father did not love either, I spent a lot of time trying to cover up my lack of desirability. Decades dissembling—trying to appear loved—so no one would know.

Yet, I was surrounded with love. Love flooded experiences that I did not name as love. These things presented themselves all the time. They sought me. I sought them.

Adnan writes that not all her passions in life were for people: a*lthough popular belief holds love in its most common use as romance or passion, it does not need to be that reductive.* Though I have heard this idea before, Adnan made it wholesome. I had been raised that love for things was wrong. Love for things was a moral failing. I was inordinately attached to things: my animal poster, my doll, books, a shirt with an embroidered flower. I gripped them because they were objects, because they were concrete. They could not retreat from my love.

In Geneva, NY, where I was born, there were stone steps that descended a steep hill into the small downtown; from the top they had a beautiful view of Seneca Lake. They were a dark red color, the kind of stone that leaves a smoky red dust on your clothes if you rub against it. I used to walk up and down those steps often because they led to the town ice rink. An extreme loneliness led me to the rink in the winter because I wasn't happy there. There was a gang of girls that pushed and kicked me. I did not fight back. It was during a time of great alienation at school, which had started in kindergarten and lasted until seventh grade when we moved to another town.

On one of these days returning from skating, I had a powerful experience at the top of the steps. At the time I called it *God.* I remember the way the sidewalk looked beneath my feet, the tiny grains in the slab of cement, with sparkling specks scattered throughout, tiny black dots, and smooth gray pieces with fossil imprints. I sat on the top step and looked over the water, and I had a sudden awareness of prayer as a dialogue between myself and some other. This other was not a body or hand, but was nevertheless *in there* listening. I remember feeling startled.

The building beside the steps was mysterious, made of the same red stone and forbidden to women. It was one of those societies for men and I never saw anyone enter or leave. Across the street was my favorite park. In the center was a naked stone lady seated in the center of a square fountain. I used to climb her, but her body was made in such a way that there were no footholds. When I sat in her lap, I would slide off and had to cling to her waist, which also was impossible to embrace. She was large. Her thighs, belly, and legs were one single piece of stone and the etched indentations that separated them eluded grasps.

Etel Adnan was tethered to the sea by her mother. Her mother, beside her on the rock, gave her an experience of love that she lived with her entire life. It was not simply the sea and its expansive freedom, but the safety of her mother's love, the quiet presence of her mother on the rock while she swam.

I have curtailed many of my loves and pushed them away. I didn't want the shame of having my love rejected.

Adnan describes painting Mount Tamalpais every day, writing a book to come to terms with it, even physically orienting herself in its presence. My heart hurts with envy. She allowed love to enter, she followed her desire. Love for Mount Tamalpais overtook her life. She lived in a house *filled with its view*. She painted nothing else for years until she *couldn't think of anything else*.

Did Adnan's immense capacity for love begin with her mother? Love for her mother permeates her poems as much as linden trees.

During the time that I had no school friends, I developed a relationship with two old ladies who lived a block away: 70 year old Pat Natti and her mother Mrs. McCloud. What I felt for them was love. Unlike other loves, I freely cultivated it. They did not retreat from my love, from its need and intensity.

Mrs. McCloud was in her early 90s when I knew her. I still have her picture, inscribed "To my dear friend, Jessica" on the back. She and I used to sit daily on the front stone stoop and watch the road. She usually had an afghan thrown over her. We rarely spoke. I remember distinctly the soft skin of her hands, like milk. She had a puffy halo of white hair. I washed her lunch dishes. Afterward, she'd ask me to sing "Jesus Loves Me."

There is an ugly memory from that house. During those years I used to attract dogs. Not in a friendly, furry way, but in an aggressive way. I was bit at least three times as a child because fear permeated my whole body, all the time. I startled and jumped easily. Dogs could smell me. I could be in a pack of other children and a dog on the other side of a yard would make a bee-line straight for me. Once outside the corner store, a dog broke off its rope to bite my leg.

An unloved body moves hesitantly, lightly. It has no foundation. An unloved body attracts cruelty.

Pat Natti's eldest daughter came to visit and brought a dog that she and her husband had adopted. It was a german shepherd and it had been abused. Later we learned that the abusers were children. The dog was shut behind the basement door when I came over.

We were in the kitchen when Roman, that was the dog's name, burst through the door and ran straight for me. He latched onto my calf and started tearing it up. Pat Natti was not strong enough to pull him off. I remember her pained voice, her head tilted upward. I can still see her behind me, pulling on the dog's collar to get him off me while calling her daughter's name. I remember looking over my shoulder and feeling sorry for her helplessness. I still have a wishbone-shaped scar behind my knee.

I also loved, during this period, a handful of shells that I bought at a garage sale. We lived far from the ocean, but a babysitter had given me a book called *The Shell* with color photos. I matched the shells to the images. I used to stroke and kiss them. I held some of them to my ear to listen to their whispers. Their whisper was my own rushing blood. Their whisper was God. I kept them in a shoebox that I carried from apartment to apartment as we moved.

Adnan describes the first time she entered the Louvre and saw the Venus de Milo. She fell in love: *And then I turned and saw the Venus de Milo. The statue of white marble was standing there, rising or bending according to one's place, seemingly larger than life. How long did I stand there, looking at her? Time, certainly, didn't matter. I was alone. We were alone. My eyes went over her body, which is between flesh and stone—stopped here and there, discovered her curves destined to both attract and keep at a distance, wondered at the mystery of such a presence, alive and still made of marble, meant to not be touched but dreamed about.*

Objects contain a life force. We alter them with our gaze and touch. Their presence alters us. Shells in particular hold the trace of the animal who once lived inside them, who smoothed their sides with wet flesh, who carried them as if they were a part of the body.

Where the body ends and objects begin, there is a transference.

When Mrs. McCloud was dying, her family gathered around the bed. They let me stay in the room. She gestured and mumbled as she lay. Her daughter tried to guess what she wanted. Her granddaughter kept bringing her different things, which she pushed away with her hand. I went to her shelf and stood on tiptoe to reach the black and white photo of her husband. I brought it with that particular 5 year old pride or maybe it was the know-it-all carriage of my body that I knew was repellent to my mother. I handed her the framed photo. She pressed it to her chest, she shut her eyes.

In elementary school I did not swallow my food. I did not speak or eat in front of my classmates. My food I threw away. Now they call it self-selective mutism. Two years ago I had a student with this diagnosis. We looked in each other's eyes. She never spoke. After every class she stood at my elbow with her sketchbook open to the drawing of a wolf. Some days the wolf had tears, claws, a collar with spikes, text bubble that said, *Why did you abandon me?* She held it open at my side even if I moved around the room to help another child. She held it open at my side, so what the wolf had been through I would know.

She moved when I moved, the drawing between us. Her sketchbook brushed my arm. The drawing tethered her to me, and I heard her without words, the way I had once heard God.

Alice Friman

Speaking of Diversion

On the day we buried Daisy,
the hearse had to stop for gas.
Our limo with its trail of cars
followed, crowding into that
Shell station not daring to be
separated from Daisy–the only
one who knew where we were
heading and how to get there.
The driver apologized profusely.
Some pimpled underling at the
Paradise Funeral Home where
We feel your pain forgot his job.
Daisy didn't mind, but we, stuck
in that big black car, laughed uneasily. Her grandson told jokes,
her son chuckled over a hangnail
which had irritated him all week,
while I, a mere daughter-in-law,
fought to keep my face straight.
But Daisy remained still, having
absorbed all the world's patience

by now, now that all the funeral
fuss was over. Perhaps the fact
that she was the star of the show
made her feel–in a strange way–
responsible or embarrassed. She
was always feeling embarrassed.
Well, all that was over now too,
wasn't it? Some things are hard
to wrap one's head around. Like
this gas business. I mean to say,
could you ever, in the depths of
your wierdest fantasy, imagine
such a thing as a hearse running
out of gas? Shakespeare would
have written it in as comic relief
and let it go at that, even with
our Daisy dolled up in her best
going-away clothes, patient as
a post and not even capable of
appreciating the joke. In truth,
I never thought his comic relief
was so comic or much of a relief.
Take the drunk porter in *Macbeth*,
Act II, Scene III, if you're tempted
to look it up. The very moment
doom's bang, banging at the gates
and treason's twisting its bloody
knife, the very moment prophecy
cackles, grinding its gears, greased
by the sweat of the gibbet rope,

he's off and running at the mouth–
a blithering fool, a clown, while
the audience, stuck in their seats,
titter uneasily, exactly as we were
doing, stuck in that big, black car,
anxiously waiting for the hearse's
tank to fill so we and the cars behind us could finally find the place
where in the end we were all going.

Alice Friman

The Elusive Art

I sing of dance, the body's joy
that fades to memory as soon as
it's over. Whether leap, arabesque,
arched back flashing in the spotlight,
or you in the privacy of your room—
pirouetting, pointing a toe—there
where no one can see. Just you
and the music wrapped in each-
other's arms. Making a dance.

I remember Nureyev, how he spun,
the sweat spraying off his body
baptizing the front rows. The fling
of it, the salt of it—proof
of the body's triumph—each spin,
each leap wrenched from the knot
of himself. And why, but to bestow
beauty, gifting us by his streaming effort
to make the effort sublime.

I too used to dance, after school
when no one was home, twirling
until I felt the music quicken in my body
the way you feel the big drums
coming down the street in a parade.
That's it, isn't it? The music, a part of you,
and you straddling it, riding it, as I did,
making myself half girl, half horse—
a dancing centaur, a magic thing.

Hollie Dugas

Love Poem to the Wicked Witch of the West

You had me at *I'll get you my pretty.*
Wordless, I watched you generate
your ball of lightning in the sky
like a tiny sun-spell—and I knew
I wouldn't be going back home.
If it's shoes you covet, come here
and skin their soles from my feet.
You can hold them all you want—
your darling familiars, they are
slithering across the yellow
pavement like the drops
of my heart to you.
You are the dark and coy thorn
in my poppy-dreams. The promise
of my name entering your spooky,
cavernous mouth and taking shape
gets me winding down hell-paths
where I'm sure to encounter
your blood pact. Let's put aside
the digging of one another's
graves and melt our shirts off.

Love Poem to the Wicked Witch of the West

This heavy bucket of water I lug
around is only foreplay. Give me
your tongue like a little bat.
I'll disappear with you
into your black bubble,
find a hundred vile ways
to become possessed by you.

Doug Ramspeck

Green Coat

There were the holy smells of oil paint
and linseed and turpenoid.

And there was an easel by the window
and a pottery wheel.

In one painting, the subject had been dissected
into cloud parts, the face floating away.

And there was a view, out the windows,
of angled sunlight dimming each evening

into a fine smoky dust that reminded me
of the sacred freight of years, the way

the hours disintegrate in the fingers.
And wind seeping through the windows

sounded like the earth was sharing its secrets.
And because the house was in the mountains,

gravity and the elasticity of time
caused the seconds to move infinitesimally

more quickly than in the valley.
And my dreams each night were a clerical filing

of memories and the random firing of neurons
the brain struggled to decode.

And always there was a strange equivalence
of things: the sunlight becoming the rain

becoming the translations of the wind.
And what about the vultures that flew up

from the roadside like mystics? Then the days
were snakeskins disintegrating in the fingers.

And sometimes, in the late afternoons,
there was thunder in the distance, some repetitive

and soothing prophecy of fissuring sky.
And there was a painting of the earth giving birth

from between the surreal altars of its legs.
And, come winter, you wore your green coat.

It ventured past your knees. It had large, round
buttons you rarely fastened.

And often the coat was draped over the back
of a chair in the studio. Or the coat was hanging

from a hook in the kitchen or slung over an arm
as we looked up through the windows

at the hallucinogenic labyrinth of the clouds.
And the coat smelled like it had been formed

from woodsmoke and cigarette smoke and years.
And cigarette smoke rose above us

like a cuneiform language on our afternoon walks.
And the wind flapped the coat like an occultation.

Nicole Rollender

You Can't See Ghosts

You can't imagine how many times my parents used that line on me. Yes, an old couple lived in this ivy-covered split before us & yes, they died, but they don't sit next to your bed whispering like gyroscopes. Even if you could see the man's black eyes, heavy brow and hawkish nose, he wasn't really there, though the darkness congealed in his wrinkles. The dead don't let you forget them, like Uncle Ziggy sitting in his leather armchair when we got back from his funeral. (Remember when I triumphantly yelled, "Uncle Z beat the Grim Reaper!" and you dragged me from the brownstone?) Or Old Papa John, who didn't realize he crossed over for a while & couldn't find the light switch? Or Aunt Blanche, whose ashes sat on a dresser next to her Lenox swan for two years waiting to be buried, while she'd show up red-eyed & pissed off? Or Uncle Ken, who everyone called "a good man, gone too soon, too fast," passing by with an eagle-winged

spirit? But, remember, none of this is real & you can't see ghosts. Because the spirit's locked up like a little beating hummingbird clock next to the spleen & when it's released, it's gone. A puff. A snow squall. A poof of Grandpa's cigar (he also came back, jaunty stepped, from purgatory on his way to paradise). But you can't see ghosts, especially not the ones who die by suicide. Not the clothing designer who sublimated Baroque art onto silk scarves and called you at work, raving about damaged hearts & getting angry when you hung up. And you didn't have that dream three nights in a row where he put a gun to his head in a garage & pulled the trigger. (Though it's true, on the third morning his sister called to say he shot himself in the head in his garage & he died.) The problem is, your Eternal Rests can't help him now, unless he wasn't in his right mind. The death-by-hangings are among the most tormented & they want to show you how they looped the rope

around their warm necks. The what-if moment in between kicking away the chair & not. Sometimes they regret it. Sometimes they don't. Sometimes during a Halloween party, they show you how they did it in the attic. They squeeze a length of rope around their own neck so hard it burns yours. Sometimes, the homeowner says, "Yes, the former tenant did hang himself. We didn't want anyone to know." But the secret's out. They tell you where you can visit his grave. And you still can't see ghosts. But sometimes, this is the night your husband says, "That's it," & converts, taking the Confirmation name George, for the saint who slayed the dragons that everyone says aren't real & you can't see.

Andrew R. Touhy

Arms

Something's under the bed. Progress? He was three when a skunk, giant or perhaps the size of a man—I can't know how my son imagined the creature—came to the loft door and knocked. Did we open up? Did it force its way in? The fear seemed to begin and end with the outsized skunk suddenly on the step. Knocking. As any visitor would.

A whisper: Will you check?

Me: There's hardly room for anything scary.

Why?

Well, I said, in compartment one is your jammies bin. And you wear a lot of jammies. In compartment two we have the Millennium Falcon filled with all of your Star Wars guys—and you have an army of those. Two Lukes and even two Vaders, last I counted. In compartment three, your adventure toolkit and the sack of silver coins TT gave you and your green money box, which is bursting we all know with hundreds in unearned allowance.

Daddy.

Is it more than that now?

Monsters can fit anywhere, he said. I have a bad feeling tonight.

A hand found mine under the covers, closed tight around my pinky.

What bad feeling? Did something happen at school?

I'll say after you check.

Polished concrete floors looked snazzy in the day. Ours—jug-wine brown—shone sleek as a red sports car in the afternoons, when bathed in sun from the trio of soaring windows. But dead of winter, and you've made your kid's room out of a narrow walk-in closet, they are little more than cold hard slab under the knees.

I poked in this nook, that. I rummaged—a mild rummage. I stared, not that he could see me seeing nothing. But I wanted him assured. I wanted to say with heart that I'd been thorough.

Then I looked, really. Maybe something was there.

It was utterly black darkness. Not the kind like in your mind, behind shut lids, where light inevitably finds its way to tint your thoughts. Here was vast, empty, forever-eating dark spread before me, bending around me, it seemed, drawing me forward. I kept my eyes on it. I felt its tug on my insides. It could take me at any moment, I knew. This force could gather me up and pull me apart and carry my bits and pieces off to where there was no me, never a me.

I put a hand in, I don't know, a foot from my nose. Waved. There wasn't anything. Just space. Air, of course, which we touch every second but can't feel, or feel touching us, right along with all those other subatomic whatnots we're so smart about but forget, or ignore, largely. And then there's the stuff we know zilch about, particles they now think hold the world together like mortar, except that they're the bricks. Bricks that float through our bones or Earth's nickel core all the same, in and out of black holes just as they please.

So what do we know about what's out there? That is to say, *right here.*

Could be dragons. Ghosts. Boogeymen. Why not. Could be Santa Claus, the Easter bunny, werewolves, zombies, aliens, ourselves—

I reached all the way in.

Anything? came a whisper.

An icy chill shot through me.

Daddy?

I found him through his dinosaur comforter. He'd drawn it taut across the bed, up to his chin. I got to my feet, gave each aching kneecap a squeeze, then slid back under the covers. Quick came the steamy press of his body to my side, warm running down my hip and thigh like the old days when he wet the bed.

Just us, I said.

You're cold!

Not beside you I'm not.

He pressed harder. You checked everywhere?

Well, there's under the bed and—you live in a closet.

You weren't afraid?

Funny, I was. Just being older doesn't make you any less scared, I guess.

When you were little, I meant. You weren't afraid of anything as a kid.

Oh, that's not true, I laughed.

Big strong Daddy?

There were plenty of monsters in my room.

There are no monsters you said.

In my head—monsters I made up. Stuff I imagined.

Which ones?

I thought honestly about this but came up short. Then I remembered the night I stayed up watching one of those Nightmare on Elm Street movies. I must have been in middle school, ten or eleven years old. The living room in our house had this big picture window. When you turned off the television all that glass lost its reflection. Everything out front—the porch and driveway, the island of lawn running to the street—came clear into view, suddenly alive in the dark.

It'd stormed earlier that night.

The drive was wet still, a slick black. A leftover wind worked over the thinnest of the palm trees, their ragged fronds whipping at themselves. But the sky was clear. The moon full, low. And there was Freddy, standing beside our tan station wagon. He wore his beaten fedora and that ratty striped sweater, of course. But his arms were off. This came straight from the movie, the scene that really got my blood going. His arms were extra long and oddly bent, like the shadows cast by arms, or the trunks of those blowing palms.

He opened them wide and stepped forward and the arms grew longer, and kept growing longer, as he moved toward the house.

I couldn't budge. It was all I could do to keep from bolting to my room. But I couldn't budge. It was like I was glued to the couch.

Even the remote control stuck to my hand.

When I looked up he was on the porch. He was inside. Ugly face sneering through those horrible burn scars, cackling, and I screamed for God. *This* he said—drawing sparks from the wall with the razory nails of his glove—*is God.*

There was a man with long arms, I told him.

How are long arms scary? he asked.

They aren't, I said. He wore a leather glove. Listen. I'm a bad parent if I tell you about him. You don't need any more fuel. You can watch the Freddy movies yourself when you're old enough. Bedtime.

His name's Freddy?

Bedtime.

The reason I think skeletons aren't creepy—

Skeletons now?

He said, I just need to say this last thing. The reason they aren't so creepy—and I'm getting a little worried thinking about them but—they don't have a brain, right? How could something without a brain hurt you?

I can't argue with your logic. Bedtime.

What about that?

That is still bedtime.

But, Daddy, I'm serious.

You'll need to be more specific with your seriousness.

On the door, he said. I think it's a scorpion or some kind of scorpion-snake.

Those I believe are Mardi Gras beads. You found them someplace . . . Live Oak Park. We hung them there on the coat hook long ago.

I found a chicken bone too that day, crawling with ants. Do you remember The Darkest of Dens?

I had to laugh. Lord knows the hours I spent watching him and his cohort thrash around under that footbridge, little preschool boots and slickers covered in mud.

You were brave ogre hunters.

He was a troll.

Ogres or trolls, brave the same. Not that you aren't now.

I didn't have to think about it then, I just knew I was fine. It was a game.

You know what I think? Maybe bravery takes practice. Instead of hiding from a fear, and feeding it, you run to it. Run *at* it. At least then you know what you're up against. Otherwise you imagine anything—you think everything's out to get you, buddy.

What about behind my stuffies hamper?

Kid, I sighed. There's nothing there. It's flush in the corner against the wall. Full of all your stuffed animals, starting with Momma's old polar bear.

It doesn't have a nose.

You can see that in the dark?

It makes him look like a creature that wants to eat me.

Not having a nose doesn't change his diet, I said. Plus he's been noseless since Momma was a girl.

Not true. Pirate bit it off.

Pi-pi?

When you went to work and forgot to lock his crate. He also ate the pocket off Momma's nice jacket and poetry book you left on the coffee table.

I don't know if all that happened. Not on the same day anyway.

Uh-huh.

Then look no further. Pirate's our monster.

Daddy.

I'll take the bear from the room.

No—

His arm swung like a gate across my chest. The weight of it, which is to say his strength, surprised me.

We've had a lot of late nights. Let's settle our mouths now and go to sleep.

His arm softened then drew back. I could hear him sucking at his checks. Then he was yawning, or blowing on something, and I remembered his whistle. I've tried to teach him, the same way my father taught me: Wet your lips, say *Chubby bunny*, and blow. But his mouth always makes the *ch* of chomp, and he's all but dropped the habit, except when too tired to help it.

Last last question? he asked.

It better not be a glass of water.

No. I'm not thirsty.

You have to use the bathroom, I said.

I went already.

Ask it then.

Remember you said before, that you were afraid—what of?

Mm. That's a longer story than we have time for. I'll say in the morning over pancakes, if you still want to know.

But if I forget.

You won't.

His body came away from mine as he shifted around for a comfortable position. He slapped, right beside my ear, at the pillows. Finally, after a while of shaking legs, I put my hand on his knee.

In a whisper: Last last last question.

You promise, he whispered back, to stay after I'm asleep? The whole night.

I promise I'll stay until you're asleep. We'll see after that.

You're a good daddy, he yawned and, turning to the wall, pulled the covers with him.

A few sighs later his breath thickened, grew ragged. I closed my eyes and saw the glow-in-the-dark moon and stars on the ceiling of my room. How I picked them off one day when I was hanging rock posters—too grown up for that sort of thing. I'd start with those tomorrow. We'd stick them on together after school. He could make his favorite constellations. They sell all the planets, even demoted Pluto. The closet had no electrical outlets, but I could mount a little battery-operated nightlight on the baseboard. We'd grab that at the store too.

Then it was quiet over there.

Slow at first, then at once, I got up and stood leaning over him. A sweet bready smell rose from his head. He wasn't feverish, just damp with sweat. His breathing steady as the sound of distant traffic.

I heel-toed lightly to the door. The knob was tricky, not that there was a trick. It squeaked no matter how you twisted. A knocking started in the wall he shares with the neighbor beside us. When I turned it became banging that climbed up and spread across the ceiling. It was pipes; she was showering, or washing dishes. It's an old building, a first-wave conversion full of dated plumbing I knew, and retold myself, though not before that cold chill ran through me again, like ice poured on my back.

But the shiver was part embarrassment, too. My body's way of rehashing something I said that was so stupid as to be shameful.

Practicing our bravery? And how do you run at the monsters when they're on the inside? When it's more like they're bursting out of us? Are us? And long arms are scary. They can reach you anywhere. They get into your head when you're awake, and when you dream. They get into your gut, your heart. They can wrap themselves around you and squeeze no matter how far you go or how fast you run. Though I suppose they work the other way also, or the same way, when they're good and loving.

I lifted the covers and pulled him in.

Daddy his voice hugged.

John Gallaher

Time Is an Emotion

My adoptive parents told me my birth-father died on the
    4th of July.
It was my one fact. It grew big as a house
I could curl up in. Later, when I was in high school,
I got a picture, gray and airless as the moon. Later,
I got upset and ripped it into four strips. Then I regretted it,
and taped it back together. And I know what this means.
    It means
I'm upset. It means dying is the great ephemeration. All
    that is us
goes on to live some other way, in pieces, for a teenager
to pin to a wall above their desk. The father frozen
    in amber.
Dear ornamental father. Me and my constituents
will be over here, talking things over, we say,
but to others it sounds more like
                                        "Hi, my name is."

They were almost right, my parents. He died on July 9th.
That's pretty close. If I were writing a poem about America,
maybe I'd leave it. It's OK to do that in art. But not in life,

and I'm trying to be more "in life" these days.
I don't remember what I was thinking when I ripped
the picture.
I think it was a version of what I was thinking while I
taped it
back together. That there's a portal that opens
in photographs,
and for a moment you're on the other side. Like imagining
the distance
of the universe. Uncanny time. Diorama of ancient Rome.
Colorized, motion-corrected film of a walking tour
through Paris, 1895.
The past has a present for you. How it felt,
watching fireworks all those years, thinking fireworks
are death,
and then losing that too, to the indistinct 9th of July.
A Tuesday.

Andrew Hemmert

Should All Our Greatness Be Forgot

And now New Year's Eve again, this reminder that the
  world doesn't need us
to go on, that the stoplights will keep changing and
  the drivers

will keep ignoring them, flooring it through the reds, the
  traffic cameras
will take their scandalous pictures until a strong
  enough storm

snaps them from their perches and sends them crashing to
  the blacktop.
For my money the blue jay is the bird with the
  greatest distance

between the beauty of its body and the ugliness of its song.
I hope to be the opposite of the jay, though most days I
  open my mouth

and statistics pour out like mudslides. I am wondering again
what subsequent disaster will be enough to end us.

Until then I have champagne, and gulf shrimp for a boil.
    Until then
there is the descent of the glittering man-made meteor
    into Times Square.

"Should all our greatness be forgot" is how I used to think
"Auld Lang Syne" went. I've sang a lot of songs I didn't
    really understand.

The stubborn morse code of Christmas lights beats red
    and green
against the evening. I am listening, I am listening for
    the sound

of something shifting in the air, though it's just our
    latest number
running its course. There's only so much you can do

with numbers. Whereas a song can show you a train
    trailing gray smoke
over the prairie in the last dusk of a number's world.
    I am trying

to unlearn my allegiance to numbers. I am trying to learn a
    kind of faith
despite my finite nature. I wanted to dedicate this to
    the man

who ran the red today and almost killed me. As I slammed
    on my brakes

and jolted against my seat belt like a crash test dummy in a
trial run,

I could see him scrolling on his phone—just like me,
more a citizen of the internet than of physical experience.

That's how it feels anyways. I resolve to visualize the feeling
of standing in a cold river as my clothes fill up with what
must be snowmelt,

at least here in Colorado. I resolve to get a little dirt under
my fingernails
and leave it there, so that I can take a bit of this year

into the next one with me, little time capsule the color
of rust.

Grant Clauser

Taking Down the Lights

Because every celebration
has to end, lest we get too easy
with joy. Because even a string
of twinkling bulbs around
the house or over the trees
can't change that cold rain
turns to ice, and even small
lights take energy, draw something
out of us until we've had enough.

Foot by foot I pull the wires off
the eaves, drop the strings onto
salted sidewalk and frozen grass.
Our shrubbery returns to mere landscaping
letting winter just be winter, not
a soft gloss we gaze at for a while,
a story we made up from childhood.

Each year feeds into the next
like small rivers flowing into
larger ones. Days of joy. Days

of not. Eddies that swirl for a while
then disappear. You've lost people.
I've lost people. We take the lights
into our hands, pack them away
until the darkness calls them back
again, when we've almost gotten
used to living without them.

Terri Brown-Davidson

Moonlit Cranes by the Rio Grande

I wake up, cold-boned, and it's all about loss.
The cranes, sleepy, shift, silvered
And glittering, wings, beaks, eyes
Phosphorescent under a broomal moon,
The crepuscular necks thrusting
Elongated through fog swarming over them
In bright-struck, vaporous wisps, so
Swiftly I'm breathless, loving
The mind-siphoning these birds induce,
The sleight-of-hand proffered by shadow-blacked
Eyes unflinching, insensate,
As were yours when you left me,
Your face under a sheet that I refused to pull back.

Dagne Forrest

Residuum

i

My hand hovers over a stick of butter in the fridge, hesitating. The brightly lit shelves of the fridge seem full, but I know how quickly that can change. Abundance is reduced the moment the stick of butter or the cup of sugar is committed to the bowl, abundance is reduced just by living.

I've always loved the final steps in baking, of taking a rubber spatula and scraping the last of the batter from the bowl. It's satisfying to think nothing will go to waste, although there are always some paper-thin remnants that even the spatula can't quite resolve. It would take a tongue to ensure that truly nothing went to waste, a step I always stop short of.

ii

It's been months since I could hug my mother, but we talk on the phone and share snippets on Whatsapp when she doesn't forget how to use it. The pandemic has been merciless to so many, but it's different for someone at the end of her life.

Losing friends at a regular rate could be somehow absorbed when my mother could still meet up with her pals for tea, for walks, for laughter. My mother is a profoundly social person, her life has been all about other people in a way that I can't say my own has been. I'm far more solitary; friendships are sparse but meaningful.

Our very different temperaments can't help but show at times and it's led to friction, a friction that I end up feeling somehow rests with me. Why can't I be softer, less judgmental? Her frequent assertion that she and her peers lived at the best possible time on the planet can't help but grate. She doesn't seem to understand that her children and grandchildren really don't want her pity and I still haven't worked out a kind way of explaining this. Born in 1942, she's too old to be a boomer, but she has the boomer's sense of entitlement, of always wanting and expecting more, including of life itself.

One day when we talk she's tearful, down about a dear friend who is dying of cancer. She complains that her friend is *only* 78. This irritates me profoundly. Is it possible that she's forgotten that my youngest was born with serious, complex heart disease? That every milestone in his short life has been a kind of miracle that reshaped the very idea of life expectancy for us? "Only 78," hits a nerve, a deep and sensitive one, though I don't take her to task for it. I just briskly remind her that to make it to nearly 80 is pretty great, there are no guarantees of more, and certainly no promise that extra years will be enjoyed in rude good health.

Advanced age brings with it a certainty that things will start to fail, even for the most ebullient among us.

iii

In late February, a year into the pandemic, I drive to the hospital where my youngest child was born nearly twenty years ago. It's a milestone hospital for me, the place where that same child was diagnosed with a murmur that turned out to be serious heart disease, the place where my father died suddenly at 63, two weeks before my son's first open heart surgery as an infant.

I'm a year overdue for a mammogram and not looking forward to it. I have no idea what it's like for someone more abundantly endowed, but, as someone with small breasts, I'm keenly aware of how hard the tech must work to scrape the breast tissue into position, to be able to catch it properly between the plates.

It reminds me of that rubber spatula circling the bowl in ever tighter arcs, the search for leavings that shouldn't be missed if it can be helped. I feel inadequate somehow, reminded of my own waning abundance. A life lived is always reducing, waning, thinning, and there is nothing like a medical test to remind one of this.

iv

I'm conscious of not having chatted with my mother in a while, I get too caught up in work and wrangling, as I call the time I spend helping my youngest to stick to routines and finish high school online. I'm spread too thin as I also try to find time for my own interests.

She surprises me by revealing that her partner had been hospitalized with pneumonia recently. Why didn't she tell me? I scold her as gently as I can, realizing that she's just been doing what she can to cope.

Her partner is still in rough shape, undergoing tests and struggling with feeling unwell, so we agree we'll talk more regularly, she'll keep me in the loop. I say "Mum, you know he's nearly 86," wanting to open up *that* conversation, but it's not the time, it's almost too late to be the time. When we're faced with an end we can see coming, we just want to keep scraping the bowl. I understand that.

v

If you look up at the night sky, it's odd to think that cosmologists have been concerned that our universe is expanding too quickly. Familiar stars seem so stable, perched right where they should be. How can our universe be picking up a little too much speed, like an uncontrolled freight train or a run of bad luck?

Many of those same people now also believe that our universe is lacking in abundance, that it's somehow too thin. More specifically, they see our universe as decidedly less clumpy than it should be. This immediately makes me think of batter, brings me back to the kitchen and that bowl.

Seeing the fabric of our universe as though it could be the perfect pancake batter, not to be overmixed, some small lumps absolutely a good thing, is odd but is something I can grasp. It's almost comforting to think of our own small planet and the other bodies in our solar system suspended in some wider cosmological batter or dough.

The search for "enough" matter in the universe is an undeniably strange one. It reminds me of my mother and her love of what's recently become known in pop culture as Swedish death cleaning. For as long as I can remember she has lived to throw things away, culling cupboards, drawers, and shelves on a regular basis.

Once my brother and I had moved out and made lives of our own, she took to gathering up the contents of waste baskets and the kitchen garbage in our homes when she visited, only able to settle for a visit once she'd taken a full bag outside. It was as though she'd recalibrated the weight or mass of our home universe, and balanced it in a way that she could accept.

More recently she took to shifting the leavings from her own home into mine. She'd show up for a short visit and leave behind a bag with various bric-a-brac from her home that she thought we might need. A tea towel from a trip she took to Newfoundland several years ago. Kitchen gadgets, tools, an extra jar of something from her pantry she feared wouldn't get used.

The pandemic forced a pause on this redistribution of her stuff, something I welcomed as I'd run out of ways to tell her we didn't need anything, which I dislike having to do. It all feels a little too much as though I am saying I don't need her, when that's not what I'm trying to say at all.

vi

The pandemic has stolen a year or more of the time I have left with my mother, who is nearly eighty and clearly starting to slow down. While our relationship is complicated, we've been close in our own way. I've always had her in my life and she was a huge help when our kids were small.

It's not just the unnaturalness of staying in touch only via phones and screens, with the odd outside visit when we could make it work. It's the skipping of key milestones, like the loss from an injury when you sense a permanent slipping away of something you'll never quite get back.

The first Christmas under Covid was also the first time in fifteen years that we didn't have my mum and her partner along with his three much younger sons from his second marriage over for a day-long feast full of conversation and games. When we can come together again, it won't be the same. One of the sons now lives on the other side of the country, and all three have reached phases in their lives where visiting us won't make sense in the same way.

The December before the pandemic began my mum and I were able to take a weekend away together in a small town near where I live. We went to craft fairs, window shopped on the town's main street, and enjoyed meals together, catching up to the point of silence. The heritage inn that we stayed at is about to close its doors, reverting to a private home. A shop where she bought a red woolen hat for me on impulse now stands empty, a victim of the pandemic's brutal treatment of some small businesses.

It feels a lot like the carpet is being rolled up behind us. We've reached a point in our relationship where abundance no longer lies ahead of us, it only exists when we look back. I guess that's something we're both having to reckon with, each in our own way, and neither one of us wants it to feel as though we're scraping a mostly empty bowl.

Julie Danho

The Couple in Front of Me at the Coffeeshop

It feels deep in the marrow, cellular, the way I tense
at how she leans back against his chest to point out
a streusel muffin while his hands are stroking

her hair, then tracing the thin straps of her sundress,
rubbing her bare shoulders as if she could grant
his every wish. As she talks to the cashier, he's whispering

in her ear, nervous as a golden retriever that suspects
his owner is soon off to work. They're in their late fifties,
I'd guess. He's wearing a checkered button-down

that looks like the tags were cut off today. Her face floats
under glasses her nose holds up like a huge red barbell.
While I order, they nuzzle just inches away, waiting

for their coffees, sharing quick pecks as if to release
tension before bursting. They beg for backstory—
rekindling a camp romance forty years later, maybe,

or reconnecting after a family death brought her back
to this town he never left. Something about them seems
unearthed. There is such urgent joy in their lust,

as if only frequent caressing keeps the other from
disappearing. So why this desire to pry them apart?
Two decades on, you and I still hold hands, sneak

the occasional public kiss, yet even at our fevered start
never hand-fed each other as they do, her fingers slowly
brushing the sugar from his lips. Do you remember

that piece we heard on the radio—three minutes
at the end of a Valentine's broadcast about a couple
always making out at their kid's Little League games,

and how, at first, everyone gossiped, doing their best
not to look? Back then I'd dismissed the feel-good twist:
by mid-season, all the parents, as if given permission,

were openly kissing, just like these two now lingering
by the door, pressed together tight as those neurons
poised to tell a body the moment it's been touched.

Lola Haskins

In the Fifth Year of His Parkinson's, Tim Visits Morocco

You have to see it, he says. It's amazing
how huge even one camel can seem
against the sand. He tells me he tremors
more often now, that his face has begun
to assume the mask, that its left side
no longer recognizes the right. The majesty
of the desert is that it goes on forever.

Adam Scheffler

Ode to Kentucky Horses

So each day
when I feel anxious or angry,
I prescribe myself one run
past Scroggins Stables or
Johnny Walker Stables to see
these unicorns without horns,
these cavalry without knights,
come tiptoeing across the field
towards the electric fence,
zapping alive the part of me
that was dead, tasting
the crabapples which to them
taste sweet—my city boy
meeting their country lack
of a conception of gender,
my nothing to offer meeting their
offering nothing but beauty
endlessly, the way if you put
enough horses in a state,
then it's known for them
not just for its terrible wattled

senators, and known for
the grasses they love, and that
the senators don't love, although
maybe they do—even if
the grasses aren't blue exactly,
except in the evenings
when they become a kind of
Galilee anyone can walk upon,
where maybe for a moment even
the worst of us can be graced
by being in the right time
at the right place.

Angie Macri

Familiar

A thicket meant a secret, old well or tombstones,
something buried.
No one cut thickets down. A well couldn't be filled,
the dead wouldn't be forgotten, trees decided to
make it harder,
and thorns conspired to join them. So those underneath
rested in peace even when their markers were only field
stones, and wells
kept their forms, wet or dry or some combination

as if waiting for somebody to look in with need again
or to recall shovels gone deep, then deeper. Same
with graves
but not as deep, and horizontal, sandstones pried out
become head and foot stones or infants' borders. Thickets
held singing: a child with rope and bucket, hymns to mark
passing into glory, birds we learned to name

but dared not pause to try to find by listening. We passed
such places
and knew not to enter for the snake nests

and the possibility of falling. Thickets interrupted the
    patterns of the fields,
emerald in summer, even in winter when a knot of lead
    or silver
still kept us from knowing what, graves or well, might be
    at the center.
For some things, the old told us, there was no telling.

John Bradley

Someone Once Lived Inside This: Song

Make a fly, a charming little fly that makes no sound as it buzzes by. Make another fly, just like the first one, only this fly makes such a sweet, thrumming sound, you have to sigh. Make another fly, this one neither silent nor musical, but a fly that will tickle the ankle, nibble the thigh. These meandering flies, let them mate, multiply. But soon you need something to control the silent, buzzing, biting flies. So you make a killer fly, to sever the heads of the offending flies. How quickly, how efficiently the killer fly goes about the necessary eradication. But now this fly has somehow reproduced, and there's a swarm of them biting your lip, nostril, corner of the eye. Yes, you need to eliminate these aberrations at once. So you make a fleeter, angrier insect, one that will devour the enemy whole. Your sleek assassin, it keeps diving at your eye, creeping into your ear, declaring, *Someone once lived inside this*. You leap out a back window, flee your home, your street, your town, running past the graveyard, into an abandoned factory near the sea. All the window- and door-openings you quickly brick over. Slather the bricks with thick mortar, until no speck of sky dares shine. You pace about the chambers on alert, noting how quiet, how boring it's become. One day you pull up a rotting floorboard, stare at a vein of clay in the soil. As if listening to an irresistible fugue, you take a bit of clay, a bit of spittle, a hair, and work the ball between your fingers. Back and forth, it rolls. You feel it warm; you feel it stir. As it flies away you say: *Ah, such a charming little fly that makes no sound as it buzzes by.*

Michael Czyzniejewski

The Alien Assimilates

I was brought to this planet, all Billy Pilgrim-like, though distinctly *not* paired with a gorgeous movie star. It's just me, a trough for food and water, a sleeping mat, and a tire swing. I don't have a place to go to the bathroom so I use one end of my domed enclosure, opposite from my mat. My function is to be looked at, whether I'm eating, sleeping, or shitting. Pretty easy, if I don't think about it. I used to be a welder—that was hard work.

The aliens who abducted me are more like earthlings than I would have guessed possible. They wear clothes, fix their hair in all sorts of styles, mate, raise children, and have zoos—and tire swings. They're pink as in neon pink, not Caucasian pink, with mostly black hair, but sometimes white, though not because they're older. Their mouths are longer, stretching to the ends of their chins, holding more teeth. They have considerably thicker eyebrows and I believe the males can lose their eyebrows like human males lose their head hair. Most different is the skin, which for them is more like scales, making me think they're reptiles or fish, except the females have breasts. Sometimes, on slow days, a mother will sit with her baby and feed on the bench right outside my cage. Once I got caught staring and the mom covered up, looking offended, maybe ashamed. I felt bad, but then I was like, wait, I'm naked here, in a cage. She paid money to stare at me and I have no place to go, can't cover up. When she goes home, I'll still be in my cage, never more than five yards from my last BM. I'm not the one who should feel bad here.

From my vantage point, I can see other specimens, other "guests." There's a winding brick path, lined with flowers, signage, trash cans, and a drinking fountain. At the end of the path sits this blue bird-lizard, a cross between an ostrich, a skink, and Bob Marley, long dreadlocks hanging behind its beaked head. Beyond that is some kind of red jellyfish, though it has innumerable legs and paces back and forth like a hyena. Off in the distance I hear something like a lawnmower starting, but alive. Whenever it makes its call—it only does so every few days—the zoo patrons clap and cheer, cameras flashing. I wish I could see it, just once, put a face to its roar.

I'm bathed once a week, my sleeping mat suddenly transforming into a pool, three feet deep. One second I'm sleeping, the next I'm plunging to the bottom. I slosh around, wipe off all the grime and grit and fecal matter, then climb out. Instantly, the pool is a mat again. They always get me when I'm having a good dream, like they know—my captors can be dicks. I picture them cackling as they push the button, maybe sharing the footage online (I might be their sneezing baby panda). I flip them off as I air dry, but have no idea where the cameras are, don't know where to direct my finger. I like to think they see. I like to think they know what a middle finger means.

Every few days, after hours, two of my captors visit, entering my cage. One is cool and collected—the zoo's vet—and the other is nervous, thin eyebrows, holding a rod with blue sparks popping at one end. The first time they come, the vet apologizes on behalf of her people for my situation.

"So, can I go home?"

"No."

"Can I get a bigger cage?"

"No."

"Can I have some pants?"

"What are pants?"

I stare at her. She's wearing culottes.

"I'm kidding! But no."

This space vet treats me with a respectable bedside manner, yet puts me through a battery of pain and humiliation nonetheless. Blood tests. Anal probes. All sorts of drugs. Her cohort with the shock prod sometimes helps, but never releases his rod, flinching if he hears me breathe. His name is unpronounceable, so I call him Igor.

"Hey," Igor sometimes says.

"Hey," I say back, something always going in or coming out of me.

After a few months of captivity, I develop a routine. I start to have some fun, exhibit "behaviors." I chew on my tire swing. I hop on one foot. I reach my hand down to dark places then smell my fingers—oh, how eager I am to smell my own smells! I refuse to throw my poop—that's derivative—but sometimes I walk over to my poop mound and talk to it, pretend like it's talking back. The space vet was initially excited by all this, asked questions, wanted to know what my poop was thinking. I told her the poop feels lonely. That it's cold. That it wants pants. I think she figured me out after that, but still, anything I do, she writes it down. A lot of my free time is spent thinking up new things to do to baffle her. I have a lot of free time.

The weirdest part of my predicament (though let's face it, not really) is seeing myself on T-shirts. When I was a kid, my parents took me to the San Diego Zoo and bought me a powder blue shirt featuring Ling Ling the panda, its name, *Ling Ling*, floating over its head in puffy lettering, *San Diego Zoo* underneath. I see my equivalent here, a photo of me, standing arms akimbo and naked, what appears to be my name beneath my feet. The vet lady says they've dubbed me ♋⍓♌♋●●, which translates, roughly, to "grayballs." It's a distinction, I'm told, an honorific bestowed upon an elder—they know what gray hair means on Earth. This means little alien kids know me, know the color of my ball hair, and they wear pictures of it on their chests to school and to church and to visit their grandparents. My shirt is the bestseller, me the first human they've ever hosted. I'm a celebrity. I ask again for pants, or heck, one of the shirts with my picture on it.

"No," the vet says. She suggests I never ask about clothes again.

One small grace in my life has been the DO NOT TAP ON GLASS sign posted outside my cage. I can't see it from behind but I know what it says. Every time some asshole kid pounds at my dome, trying to get my attention, a guard comes over, points at the sign, and the kid stops. I don't have much here, and they treat me like the fourth-grade hamster on the window ledge, but I have that: No tapping on the glass.

The vet and Igor come in one day and get frank: I'm masturbating too much. Used to be I'd wait until the zoo closed, when I had privacy. Once I accepted the full weight of my situation, a year or so in, I stopped caring. Field trips are my favorite. It's weird, but I'm pretty sure they have nuns, just like we do, the habit, the veil, the entire get-up, guiding their classes through the zoo. Space nuns hate it when I masturbate.

The vet asks me to stop—they're getting too many complaints. I dropped from the number one T-shirt to fourth last month—if I drop any lower, they'll stop making my T-shirts.

"And we'll castrate you."

I don't beat off for two weeks. When I do, I wait until I fall into my bath and bang it out underwater. It's not ideal, but in no time, my T-shirt bounces back. Problem solved. And I get to keep my nuts.

Beyond this hiccup, I start to settle in. I try interacting with the guests. I do tricks to get their cameras clicking, moonwalking and handstanding and general monkeyshines. I pose with kids, me on one side of the glass, them on the other. I pose with adults. I even pose with nuns. I stop talking to my poop and try to never pee until after hours. I start doing yoga, or what I think is yoga. I actually try my tire swing: It's no great fun, but I like figuring out how the rope is attached to the top of the dome—the connection is seamless, like it's all one piece. I have longer talks with the vet—I name her Dr. Jane—and find out she's married but can't have kids. She even cries a little as she tells me. I try to convince her to adopt. She tells me she's thinking about it, that she wishes I could talk to her wife. I tell her to bring her by, let me have a go, and Dr. Jane says that one day, she might take me up on that.

Me and Igor sometimes catch a ballgame after hours, him holding his little handheld up to my cage, explaining the rules to their bat-shit crazy sports. A lot of their games involve batons instead of balls. When I explain balls to Igor, their obvious functionality, he tries to understand but I see he does not.

My Earth clothes, keys, phone, and wallet have been in a museum since I got here, but Dr. Jane arranges for them to send me the photos from inside the wallet, a few shots of my nieces my sister sent me. I hide them inside of the tire, something I look at to remind me of home, something pure and good.

I've never been healthier and am close to admitting that maybe I've never been happier. I stop thinking of home and accept I will die in this cage. And I'm okay with it.

Just when I think I've achieved a semblance of peace, some zoo administrator comes to visit. I've never seen this guy before, but I know he's a bigwig because he's wearing a suit. It's got a vest and cufflinks and there's a lavender hanky in his pocket that matches, I kid you not, an ascot. His eyebrows are obviously fake, the worst eyebrow toupee I've seen since arriving on this planet. He says he has good news: They've captured another human, a female. They want me to mate with her, have a baby, and the zoo will revolve an entire marketing campaign around us. They'll make millions. I won't see any of it, of course, but I might get a bigger cage, perhaps even a second tire swing.

I am elated. I try to picture her, this woman, wonder if she's my type, but don't get ahead of myself. After two years in a space zoo, seeing all these scaly pink freaks every day, literally any human woman would do the trick. "Let the mating commence!" I say, and the head zookeeper smiles, but immediately lets the air out of the room: The female they've acquired is a baby, a newborn. My job will be to raise the baby, in this cage, in front of the whole world. And when she's old enough, I have to mate with her.

The suit explains they've done their research, know human women can get pregnant as early as nine. I'm to get started as soon as possible. Ten years from now, they want the family in place, me, my stepdaughter/child bride, and our offspring … our *first* offspring.

When I refuse to cooperate, I am told I have no choice. The alternative? They'll harvest my sperm and do it without me, and by "without me," they mean they'll put me down. The administrator is clear on this.

"And to think, we thought you'd be pleased," this suit says. "Based on those pictures from your wallet."

For days, I don't get off my mat. I don't eat or drink. I don't even stand up to pee. There's a lot of tapping on the glass, followed by what I assume is a lot of sign-pointing-to. Not that I can see: I keep my back to everyone.

The vet comes in and does more tests than usual. She asks me if I'm feeling okay. I don't answer. She runs more tests and I still won't answer. She motions to Igor, who sticks his shock stick into my ribs. I convulse, my blood on fire. I'd been tased back on Earth—I once punched my town's mayor at a beauty pageant—but this is a hundred times worse. When I stop shaking, the vet examines my pupils, listens to my breathing. She asks again if I'm okay. I look at Igor, his prod humming.

"I'm so happy, I've been at a loss for words," I say.

The vet writes this down. She nods. She says, "The human baby will be here tomorrow. Congratulations, ♋⍓♌♋●●. You're going to be a father."

That night, I contemplate hanging myself with my tire swing. I'm working on the physics when someone taps on the glass. I turn around and Igor shines a flashlight in my face. He enters my cage. He is alone. He doesn't have his prod.

"Be quiet," he says.

Igor tells me he's the one who did the research and found out human kids can have babies at nine. He says he read further, about statutory rape. About age of consent. He even gets that I'll be her dad first, that this will make it all a million times worse.

"A million at least," I say.

"Be quieter," Igor says. "I'm here to rescue you."

Igor tells me to get on my hands and knees and be still. I feel something sharp in the back of my neck, an intense, searing pain. He says he's removing the restraining chip.

"Your head would explode if you left the grounds," Igor explains. He crushes a little metal chip beneath his boot then cleans my wound.

Just like that, I walk out the cage, the first different perspective I've had in so, so long. I turn and look at my cage, at the vantage everyone's had of me—I glance at my mat and my swing and my poop pile. Good riddance, I think. I'm going home.

Igor and I sneak past the other cages, most of the other captives asleep, though the red jellyfish still paces. When it sees us, it picks up its pace. I nod when I walk by and it nods back.

I finally see the thing that makes the lawnmower noise—it's the size of a mouse, but hairless and a creamy blue. It sees us and makes its sound. It's majestic. I clap and it bows. I'm pretty sure it winks at me, but it only has one eye, so it might just be blinking.

I am loaded into a van behind the employee entrance, where Igor's comrades wait in the back. They explain they're from some kind of animal liberation cause. They look ragged and strung out and like they don't know what they're doing—in other words, it checks out. Igor, who's driving, was their inside guy. Five years in, waiting for their chance to strike, and now they've burned him on *me*, to get *me* out.

"Thanks," I say. I am truly grateful.

We drive for hours. In between singing songs, my liberators explain the kind of work they do. It's a lot like Earth's equivalents, red paint on fur coats, letters to senators, the occasional story on public radio. They tell me it's an honor to meet me, for them to free me from my captors.

"So I'm going home?"

The liberators laugh. They explain they do not have access to space travel—they had to steal this van just to pick me up.

"We're no astronauts."

I realize now the beings who have zooed me are not the aliens, not here. This is their home planet. I'm the one who's far from home. I'm the one who doesn't belong. I'm the one who's fucked.

Some time later, we stop. The back doors open, revealing Igor, flashing one of his people's gigantic, stupid grins.

"We've arrived, my friend."

I pile out of the van along with the whole gang. We're at a trailhead, at the edge of a forest. I'm thinking we're going to be picked up by another vehicle, or maybe their headquarters is in the woods, a hidden lair. There I'll live among them. Maybe there'll be other rescued species. I could be part of the cause, work behind the scenes. I imagine a situation based on mutual respect. Maybe I'd even be happy.

"Run along," Igor says. "You're free now."

I stare at him.

"No need to thank us. Just go and live!"

I shrug, still staring. "What?"

The liberators all look at each other, mumble amongst themselves.

"What's the problem?" one asks. She's wearing a me T-shirt, purple. Purple really brings out the gray in my ball hairs.

"Where do I go?"

"Wherever you want! You're free!"

The group files back into the van.

I want to point out to my liberators how I don't have food. Or clothing. Or shelter. How they didn't find me in the wild—I was abducted driving home from a Sonic, drinking a banana milkshake I'd spiked with vodka, playing *Candy Crush* at stoplights. I stay silent instead.

Igor shuts the doors. He salutes me like I'm a general and gets back into the van. They drive away and in twenty seconds, I can't see them anymore, not even brake lights.

I peer into the woods. It's pitch. I take one step onto the trail. I hear all kinds of things, sounds of unrest and sounds of warning. I take another step, then another and another. Something lands on my back, bites me, then flies off. It itches but I don't dare touch it with my fingers. I find a log and sit down, then wonder if it's even a log. I think about myself, how I won't last out here, how I'll die from exposure by morning. I start to cry, then stop, not wanting an army of curious, hungry beasts homing in on me. I whimper instead, covering my mouth to stifle any noise.

Then I think of that newborn, the little girl I was supposed to raise. Now she won't have anyone of her own kind. All she'll know is the zoo, that cage, those pink scaley bastards. I want to go back to the zoo but remember we drove for hours. Who knows what I'll run into first, if I'd even end up back at the zoo and not as something's meal. I could be shot by some jerkoff with a space gun, my head adorning the wall of a wood-paneled den. A million other possibilities seem more possible than me making it back to the zoo.

I have to try.

I stand and take a step but have lost which way is out. The bite on my shoulder starts to burn. I risk a scratch and it feels good, but when I stop, it feels much, much worse. I'm thirsty, I realize. I miss my trough and tire swing. I forgot the pictures of my nieces.

I wonder what they'll name that baby girl. I wonder if they know how to take care of her. I wonder if she'll survive.

I need to find something to drink. I need to get back to the zoo. It's starting to feel cold outside. I never should have left. I need to get back. I wish I was wearing pants.

Lauren Watel

That Summer

That summer I got my period and dreamed a man. He was tall, gray-headed and muscular, with kind serious eyes and sensitive hands, hands that could catch an egg without it breaking. Tan skin, good taste in trousers. I named him Adam, naturally, and he kept me company many a night. He laughed at my jokes. He dried my tears. He gave me treasures and never asked to be repaid. He clapped and cheered when I did well, picked me up when I fell. He brought me flowers, sent me love letters. He tied my hands to the bedpost, but only when I wanted him to. He never got angry with me, never lost patience with me, never rolled his eyes at me, never scolded me. In short, he wrecked my life, this Adam I dreamed into being. No man could live up to his promise, though I kept waiting at the door, eagerly, like a well-trained hound. Every time a man walked through, I looked into his eyes and saw Adam, and every time I learned, only too late, that it was not Adam; it was someone else, anyone else. No wonder I was so bereft. This was years ago. Now I'm gray-headed myself. Soon enough I'll have my last period, though I still sometimes dream of Adam, my first man, ruinously fantastic, heroic, as solid as ice is before you have it in your hands.

Ian Cappelli

The Stenographer Describes Their Notes

Oftentimes, when people have conversations, they simply wait for their turn to speak and proceed as if no new information had been presented. *You always forget to bring the dog bags*, presents the stenographer. The best family photographers shoot their subjects out of frame. Point the cameras at the soup stains on the kitchen wall. See the black mold crawling from the heat vents. *There's no use breaking your back cleaning: the house is like a nightshirt*, presents the stenographer. You can know, by the fresh coat of paint, the type of soup on the wall. In summer, there is gazpacho. In winter, lentil. *Cook me something I can chew on*, presents the stenographer. How much sunlight is let in could mean something. How thick the curtains. I *cut myself in the sink, leave the knife straight up again and I'll have to buy chainmail.* The spacing of clothes in the wardrobe could be shorthand for separation. The photographer, like a dreg in the reflection of the back window, appears in the speechlessness of night while the little sheepdog pisses alone: looking, doggedly, into your eyes.

Ernesto L. Abeytia

Remembrance: el Canal de Castilla (Two)

A flock of pigeons
on telephone lines
make a shadowed score.

The body shows its age
in the cracking of lips,
tired arroyos forgetting their place.

There is no escaping
this world intact.
Even the sun must rest sometimes.

Stephanie Staab

Ode to a German handyman

O Herr Schäfer
you make me feel pious.

And I'm speaking here of the way Rilke used the word
to mean devout without a trace of God, a sacred separate
from religion.

You stand in my doorway in workman's clothes
and I want to lick the metal buttons on your coveralls.

When you show up in a crisp white shirt, I picture you
standing in jeans in front of a tidy closet, selecting it.

Most of the time, you're all business. Your hands down the
drain full of my hair
or sanding an edge off the windowpane. You hardly
notice I'm there.

But you must wonder about me too because you'll slip in
a question sometimes like, "You've been in this country a
while now, no…?"

and once in a while you look at me
like you're not sure you should be looking at me.

It makes me feel romantic.
My hands can't find themselves.

O save me, I'm jealous of your other clients. I want to
lock you in
my apartment and watch you fix things. Only my things.

When you come over to repair my stove after a hard week
I'm so relieved that you're there and I can cook again

that I cry right in front of you in the close kitchen.
A cry that is trying not to cry, a series of gulps.

The next day, I apologize and you write back:
"It's not a problem at all."

And this is all going on *auf Deutsch* of course which is far
from my native language
so I have no idea how I'm coming across here.

In my imagination, it's doesn't matter
and we run into each other by chance, hiking in

the hills around here and also you have
a dog. A Labrador for a man like you. We walk together

in long loops and we let all our Teutonic formalities
    fall away.
No more Herr, no more Frau. You say

your first name out loud to me. We end up near
your farmhouse on the edge of town near the vineyards

and you invite me in and we sit on the porch
that, let's acknowledge, you built yourself.

We inch closer, circling in conversations,
the floorboards creaking, uncertain until you make

something clear. A blurry lens wiped clean.
It will all seem predetermined, like in fact it has

already happened and here we are looking back
on it and I touch your fingers, the palms of your hands.

In my dream, you kneel, admitting it.

Michael Malan

Trick or Treat

It's Halloween and the moon is full. "Double trouble," Jaylene says. "There may be some ghouls out tonight. Or big, hunky men shapeshifting into werewolves. The world, our culture—it's topsy-turvy. Everything that was nailed down has been set loose." Her face is deathly white and her fingers look like icicles. "Let's talk about something else," I suggest. "The wind on the river or the fog on the mountains. Our tender feelings for one another. The Scary School of Life, the latest Fright Night Installment Plan, or maybe the spooky wizard of Drac-in-the-Box Lane?" We open a party bag of Hershey's Miniatures and eat a few Krackles and Mr. Goodbars. The doorbell rings. Two kids dressed as Spider-Man and Captain America. I hand each a candied apple. "Ooh, sticky," the webslinger says. A large group in dinosaur costumes are coming up next—Jurassic World Fan Club. They take big handfuls from the candy bowl. Dad trails along behind, talking on his cell phone. "What? You're where? What are you doing there?" I look over his shoulder. Someone has knocked down our "We Welcome Everyone to Our Neighborhood" sign. Back inside, Jaylene and I put on our Trump and Biden masks and sit on the couch holding hands. An election is coming soon.

Michael Malan

Saying Goodbye

Isaiah was sitting on the floor reading *Meetings with Remarkable Men*. "Gurdjieff didn't think God created the universe," he said. "But He got involved after things got going. It's like God isn't omnipotent, all-powerful, but He plays a role." That made sense to me. "Look at those flowers in Golden Gate Park," I said. "God must have had something to do with that." "Yeah, those flowers are awesome," Isaiah said. We smoked a joint and listened to music on his CD player. Megadeth. Black Sabbath. "I'm going to miss this place," he said. I looked around. It was a pretty dumpy apartment. The windows hadn't been washed in, like, four decades. "When do you think this room was painted?" I asked him. "In the Sixties, I think. Look at those stains on the ceiling." The ceiling was starting to move a little, like the room was breathing gently. "I'm going to Denver," he said, "to see my sister. When it gets cold, I'll come back." I was sad to see him go. Every year one fire dies and another is reborn. Even on the darkest nights, we can see forever.

Michael Malan

Terminal Gravity

I meet Kayla at The Peacock for lunch. She's a little bitchy, but that's OK, I love her anyway. She accuses me of watching the TV on the wall above the bar instead of looking at her. I'm not looking at either her or the TV. I'm staring into space, outer space. I see a new black hole forming in the Andromeda Sector. An android waiter appears at my elbow. Kayla orders a bacon burger, French fries, and a pint of Terminal Gravity. I order a soybean burger and low-sodium V-8 Juice. While we are waiting, she tells me she has gotten an email from "a crazy ex-lover." What should she do? How should she respond? I tell her I don't know. When he returns, the waiter wants to give me the bacon burger. Kayla laughs. I look at the TV: a talking head. No sound. She's enjoying every bite of her bacon burger. Guilty pleasures? Does her husband know? I want to tell her about Jesus. Or the Buddha. *Hari Krishna. Hari Rama.* But I don't. I eat the soybean burger, watch the talking head. His hair is lifting off slowly, like a UFO before it reaches warp speed. The sky over the bar is turning red. Stars are falling on the roof, hitting the street and sidewalk, shattering like Christmas tree ornaments. "Hey," she says, "look at me."

Romana Iorga

I Took the Moon Like a Moose for a Walk

This is not a moose overhead
or a blimp picking its way through the foliage.

This is the moon. You can see it
if you really look.

A bloated fish with a hook in its mouth.
It guides and is guided by fear in disguise.

It lights up the only road I took
out of childhood.

Childhood stayed behind like a barn
chock-full of things I wanted

to forget. Pitchforks that no longer pitched
the bodies of stray dogs.

Rakes that no longer raked.
Hoes that no longer did what hoes do,

which is hoe, I suppose.
Punctured balls and that homeless plastic *pupsik*

I had to have
so I didn't eat for two weeks.

Would I be someone else had I eaten
instead? Had I shared my food

with whomever begged me for bread?
The old man talking to himself by the bridge.

The old woman at the bus stop,
too weak to speak.

Who is this stranger adrift in my body,
I hardly know. Someone

I wouldn't be friends with, if I had to choose.
A blimp, so filled with air

she's about to burst. Like fear,
she has me collared and tagged. I am hers.

How do you love
someone hooked through her mouth by regret?

I Took the Moon Like a Moose for a Walk

If this or that didn't happen, she asks,
or if it did.

I took the moon like a moose for a walk
and that was it.

Elton Glaser

Downtime in the Bucket of Crabs

The flickers of gypsy light out on the water
Break on the back of every wave.

In the Keys, it doesn't matter if those are boats
Or the moon skipping its sheen across the sea

Or the ghosts of pirates blinking from the afterlife.
Here, on the slippery edge between pleasure and crime,

Where the mangroves root in the muck, and overhead
Pelicans pilot the sky in a jawful noise,

I lift my lime and rum to the barroom mirror,
Holding myself up to myself, the air as hot and dark

As a burnt-out matchhead after the flare. There's so much
I don't remember, and even more I want to forget,

Lost in the skid and the slither and the stop.
Does the dirty jukebox make the music dirty, too,

The little lights splashing around the glass as the record
Spins me into its black trance, ache and echo of myself?

Somehow the half of me that isn't mine has gone,
And maybe gone for good, snuffed out like a summer star.

I sit downwind from the primitive scents, patio open
To the ooze and spent fuel, the sea sweating into itself,

And listen to the ring of the cymbal, the stutter of drums,
And wonder what's left beyond this joint in the sticks,

This night doused in the raw pulp of rhythm and blues.
Can every sorrow be cured by a bottle or a .44?

Is there any distance between giving up and letting go?
A brief breeze from the tide line troubles the tinsel
    and the mind.

I don't need another long night of postmortems in
    a tiki bar
To bring me back from the dead. That would take
    more than

A juju man and two blue jolts to the soul. But tonight
    I'd settle for
Waking naked one more morning in a decency
    of clean sheets.

Paula J. Lambert

This Place, Too, a Loss: Blue Whale

A blue whale's heart, they say,
is big as a Volkswagen Beetle. Because
folks on land, I guess, have no frame of reference
but the cars that carry us through our pitiful days,
place to place, mile after mile,
incessantly searching for that bigger and better something
we can call home.

The beat of a blue whale's heart, they say,
can be heard over two miles away, though it's not clear
    to me
who's listening—a boat, maybe, filled with men
weighed down by sonar devices and plastic coolers,
men with hearts small as a fist—
women, too, maybe, and other folk dreaming
of swimming inside a blue whale's ventricle because

they say that, too, you know,
that the blue whale's arteries are a tunnel
big enough to contain us,
as if that heart, big as a car, beating eight times a minute

and loud enough for most anyone's god to hear,
    wouldn't burst
our skulls from the eardrums out, drown us in the blood
she's pumping—or trying to, we the clot
most likely to kill as we sidestroke leisurely
toward the overworked chambers
of her heavy, heavy heart, thinking

this might be it at last. This might be home,
or at least a place we can stay for a while, flip, maybe,
or turn into an Airbnb, somebody else's getaway,
somebody else's home away from home, somebody else's
chance to forget about everything for a while, till
    they leave
their two-star review, of course: *seemed spacious*
but not much of a view, and be forewarned
there was some kind of really loud thumping sound
we couldn't find the source of, somebody needs to look into that,
would not recommend, and it seems best for you
to call this place, too, a loss, sell it for what you can get
or maybe just foreclose, maybe just move on.

Nathaniel Dolton-Thornton

Extinct: Cylindraspis Inepta

you've already reserved the theater's highest seats
and the hotel's top floor
you have the confirmation tickets in your pocket
windmills might miss the breeze
but you've rented that altitude indefinitely
when they see you
fall into the ocean they'll know
you own the water

Matt Martinson

Trout and Trout Remain

Taneum Creek

—Richard Hugo

I don't come here after June when rattlesnakes
come out of caves and snore on stones
along the stream, though trout and trout remain
and I am keen to harm. Yellow bells have fangs
and jack pines rattle in the slightest wind.

There's nothing special about Taneum Creek. Head east on I-90, maybe ninetyish miles from Seattle, and you won't see this narrow slip of water even as you drive over it. It's down there, sure, but good luck finding it. You will see a sign, but no creek. There's a road and bridge, but no exit. If, however, you do want to visit Taneum Creek, you have to go another two miles, take the Thorp exit, circle around on a sideroad leading you back into the not-spectacular Taneum Creek watershed.

Don't get me wrong, it's beautiful enough. And don't misunderstand me—I like creeks, I grew up on Washington creeks, but a creek is a creek is a creek: dense brush, tall trees, deer, elk, bear, trout, birds—you know, *a creek*.

Okay, fine. Not all Washington creeks are *exactly* alike. I grew up with different creeks—cricks, we called them—on the left side of the Cascades, a few dozen miles as the crow flies yet a couple hours in the car, on creeks where the underbrush is a bit thicker, as is the moss, a place where prehistoric salamanders meditated beneath granite and ferns. And there were no rattlesnakes. No, rattlesnakes are an eastern Washington phenomenon. When the summer heat comes on, which, in apocalyptic 2022, is now just as likely to be May as it is July, Washington's only rattler, the western rattlesnake, comes out to bask in the murderous sun.

Note the sibilance, with "snakes," "snore," "stones," and "stream" to remind us of the typical *sss* snake sound, but then paired with the hard "ck" sounds of "…sna*k*es *c*ome out of *c*aves," which now begins to imitate not only a rattlesnake's hiss but also the ktsch-ktsch-ktsch of its rattle, a warning of danger.

My first few years here, I was anxious, afraid of what I imagined would be a quick rattle followed by the instant, searing bite. Like Richard Hugo, I avoided the eastern Washington scrublands, fearful of fangs. But we can't cower forever. I made my way outdoors, discovering, eventually, that rattlesnakes are few and far between, that, like me, they aren't looking for trouble.

I once took some students on a hike near here, and one young woman nearly stepped on a fat, dark rattler. It gave a frantic tail shake and scooted off into the underbrush, where two of its friends were waiting. You experience that, and the initial fear of Hugo's speaker makes sense. And then it doesn't. And then the whole "They're more afraid of you than you are of them" starts to make sense.

Isn't that what Hugo's speaker is really saying here? That he doesn't actually come here after June? C'mon. How would he know what the snakes do after June if he didn't come and see for himself? Ask that question and suddenly you know it's a lark, a sardonic commentary on our fears! Oooooh, we say—he's saying in his most mocking voice—*Look at the big, scary snake, emerging from its dark, spooky cave, creeping out to, to, to…snore on a rock. Gasp!* Such a scary creek.

*

Growing up, my creek was Goat Creek, just a stone's throw west of Mount Rainier National Park, the water draining from year-round snowmelt on Norse Peak. We'd stay at my grandparents' old cabin and I'd spend long summer days with the creek's roar in my ears, a fishing pole in hand, on the hunt. For trout.

I never liked the taste of trout. I didn't like killing them. I hated putting a worm on a hook. I'm not even sure if, at that age, I enjoyed the solitude on the creek. Yet there I was, day after day, moving up and down the creek, finding calm pools beneath small falls, where, perhaps, a long, fat fish might be craving an awkwardly placed worm, magically dangling in the water. I'd stab the worm, throw its hooked form into the creek, all in the hopes that I might soon be clubbing an innocent, poor-tasting fish to death.

Once, while we were at the creek, my big brother spotted a black bear, which scampered up a tree and miraculously never came down again. The adrenaline rush of fear and excitement was palpable as we waited below, hands shading our eyes, looking up into the canopy of trees for a bear that must still be up there today.

Another time, my dad told me a story about the corral across the gravel road. This is the same corral where grandpa kept the horses he used for his hunting guide work, the same corral where my dad and his friends were practicing quick draw until one kid accidentally pulled the trigger too quickly and shot himself in the leg. In this story, there were no horses at the corral, but a doe and her two fawns were grazing. A handful of folks watched, kids in tow, oohing and ahhing the sweet spotted fawns, when, with no warning, in a non-registerable instant, a cougar held one fawn in its mouth, gone before anyone could mentally compute. It was the quick strike, he said, that was so shocking, the instantaneousness of death, like a shot in the leg or a club to the head. Or the flash of a trout in a slow pool.

Two of Hugo's lines in this poem have always bothered me: "though trout and trout remain / and I am keen to harm." The first half, "though trout and trout remain," speaks of abundance. That's one glory of nature, its abundance. It's what Jesus is referring to in all that talk about birds in the trees and flowers in the field, like when you find some untouched valley in the Cascades, full to bursting with wildflowers nobody else but you will see that season. It's what Dillard means when, for pages and pages in *Pilgrim at Tinker Creek*, she ruminates on fecundity, the seeming wastefulness in life-giving abundance in which nature seems to relish. It's the millions of salmon coming up these rivers and streams to drop unfathomable numbers of eggs. It's the Douglas fir trees above me putting out a hundred seeds in each cone, dropping a solid thousand on a good year, and only a handful of seeds will root.

It was beneath such a tree that I had my favorite fishing hole on Goat Creek, a glorious spot somehow still in view of the cabin; I could sit beneath that tree, unmoving, catch a trout, then come back and catch another the next day. I remember, one time, I must have been eight or nine, I caught four or five trout, each about a foot long. None of us wanted to eat them, and that year mom gave up on even the pretense of cooking them. So the fish sat, started to smell, and then went out with the end-of-the-week trash. I have never fished there again.

From an aesthetic standpoint, my favorite point in Hugo's poem is this break, the fact that "and I am keen to harm" comes in the next line, a glorious enjambment. If the first line speaks to an almost infinite and eternal plentitude, the second seems to take that as a challenge, like the moment when I realized the chipper-sounding "Maxwell's Silver Hammer" was about a mass murderer. It's an unexpected turn, from nature's bounty to the speaker's vile intent. It's turning a corner from paradise into a gutpunch. The poem does an about-face much like the U-turning driver attempting to reach Taneum Creek. It's nature's fecundity contra humanity's murderous nature.

Think, especially, about that word: *keen*. What a choice!

In the same way literati fans tend to romanticize the drunken antics of folks like Hugo, Cheever, and Hemingway, I've often been guilty of doing the same with the famous Raymond Carver's turn toward sobriety. If I'm being totally honest, I've always imagined him on a boat right off the Olympic Peninsula, peaceful, content, just glad to be alive and to share a moment with some poor salmon trying to make it up the Hoh River or a rainbow trout cruising up the Yakima. Folks like Carver—not to mention Duncan, Maclean, Middelton, Hemingway, Barich, Walton—they may be out for a meal, they may be out for sport, but they tend *not* to be out for violence. That's a leap. Who wants to find joy in violence? Who wants to admit it? Heck, look at keen's synonyms—enthusiastic, eager, willing—and imagine such a word aligned with *harm* of all things. It's blatantly indicative of a desire for, a need to commit, violence for violence's sake. It's a frightening moment, sadistic even. The speaker, it seems, finds pleasure in the act of brutality as an end in itself.

Is that normal? Natural? Monstrous?

I've always been haunted by a late summer afternoon adventure that took place 25, maybe 30 years ago. I was out with two cousins, deep in the woods, and massive salmon kept charging up the creek next to us, their knife-like backs slicing above the shallow creek's crest. What made us grab long, thick sticks, position ourselves in the stream, go through all the work of making barricades and detours meant to slow and deter them? I remember, still, the thrill of chasing them through the current, of swinging sticks, yelling out strategies, cursing the ones who made it out of our gauntlet. And then, when we finally corralled one into a small pool, I remember seeing the way it tried to blend in with its surroundings—and it really did—and then that final act, the three of us swinging and swinging, beating a salmon to death merely for sport, out of boredom and some deep-seated hate. I remember my younger cousin, Justin, holding the fish up afterward, not in championship or even curiosity, but rather with a blank look on his face. Somehow, as an adult, I've always acquainted that moment with the last time I saw him, in 2000, his head swollen beyond recognition at a Tacoma hospital after he got drunk and high and crashed his car alongside the Puyallup River.

We are, it seems, keen to harm.

Yellow bells, not to mention jack pines, are, though, not so eager to commit violent acts. Duh. What's interesting is that, up to now, the poem has been a bit modern-imagist, giving little more than the things-in-themselves, not far from the infamous wheelbarrow of Williams or metro station of Pound. Like all works of art, Pound, Williams, and Hugo look at the individual to, with any luck, talk about the universal. Hugo's allusions to fear and violence seem to be doing just that. Yet how do we even bring up a word like universal in a post-post-postmodern world, in a post-truth, hyper-individualized moment? How could they even do it in Hugo's day? In Pound and Williams' time?

Both Williams and Pound tried their luck at translating poems from the Chinese. Pound more famously so, obviously, but Williams, too, translated a handful of poems, published posthumously in *New Directions 19*. Regardless of the quality of either man's translations, the precision of Chinese poetic thought had a lasting influence, seeing the individual for what it is, not as an image or form of something larger, but as just a piece of the whole, looking at other pieces of the whole. Taoist and Ch'an thinking would try to teach the individual to move beyond our conceptual, language-based way of perception, which simplifies in order to group and categorize. As Emmanuel Levinas would say generations later, it causes us to totalize and, in the process, be unjust.

Yet even in Ch'an thinking, to see the individual as itself, not a representation of itself and others like it, is meant to lead to larger truths. Zhuangzi famously taught, "The fish caught, forget the net." But what's the net? Language? Thinking? Our mind itself? Yes, probably, to all three. And more besides!

In Hugo's poem, though, we flip Zhuanzi's quote around, forget the fish. But then again, of course, this isn't about fish!

Yellow bells do grow in the Taneum Creek area, but what you are far more likely to see when you come down the road is arrowleaf balsamroot, whose bright yellow flowers bloom profusely, and hang on far longer than most native flowers in eastern Washington. If you go walking out here in the summer, where the heat typically hovers around 95 as long as the sun is up, last year reaching 115 one scorching August day, everything dries up, and the crusty arrowleaves, in the breeze, sound exactly like rattles. It keeps you on your toes, and you'll find yourself leaping away from twenty rattlesnakes in one day, having never encountered any actual snakes on your sweaty two-hour hike.

It gets better: there are no native jack pines in eastern Washington, and few invasive ones, it seems, but there are lodgepole pines. I like to think this was intentional on Hugo's part, this mis-identification. We hear snakes where there are no snakes, see trees where they don't exist, and attribute violent intent to all.

Two weeks ago I read about the decimation of entire packs of Yellowstone wolves, of a mass culling across Montana as these apex predators came out of the park in winter, only to be met with armed men who'd been given permission—and were keen—to kill. The wolves are dangerous, they argue, so we have to kill them first.

Two weeks ago, Russia invaded Ukraine, a "military exercise" meant to keep Ukraine under control, to strike back first.

My uncle—a different uncle, not Justin's dad—now owns the cabin. I visited last summer. Goat Creek had been devastated, shattered beyond recognition after the entire mountain above blazed in a massive, unthinkable fire, which in turn led to mudslides, rockslides, destruction, destruction, destruction. I stood at the creek and wondered how the trout were holding up. If they even exist now, at all.

The projections aren't good anywhere up here in America's left shoulder. Rainbow trout are dying off in large numbers, the water getting too warm as the world heats up and the trees alongside the rivers and creeks burn off. Rainbow trout are beginning to only live in clumps, unable to travel or breed outside their shrinking pockets of cold. And with golden trout, living further up in the highest hills, the situation is more dire, as they hold on in tiny mountaintop ponds that shrink a bit more with each passing year.

And Taneum Creek? If you come here—and really, it's up to you—bring a garbage bag. You probably won't see a single rattlesnake or trout, but I promise you will find plastic bags and Gatorade bottles and used condoms and Styrofoam and an obscene number of spent shotgun shells.

But don't worry, the bears and cougars and porcupines and skunks and wolverines and bobcats are deep in the hills. They are not keen to harm.

Luís Miguel Nava

Rivers

Here, where we watch
it flow, the river is no more than a curtain, behind which
another river flows. What is
reflected in the first
is transfigured in the second.

The first breaks free
from the plane to which the senses
keep it clinging, the better,
thus, to enter our soul, whose
uncertain surface serves as its banks.
Put another way: the riverbanks
arrange themselves upon the coarseness
of our soul, whose hidden corners
(as Pessoa has already said) the sun does not reach.

But it isn't even needed. A single candle
in the darkness is enough
to illuminate the river
from mouth to primal source.

Rivers

It is this river, just like a door
that exists only on the inside, while on the outside
it is eaten away by darkness, that
serves us as a metaphor for time

(only the other one is literal)
and, just as in the darkness—where grass
and flowers are invisible—
fragrance grows green, and so
time, trickling away, takes on
the color of the grass: and yesterday, today
tomorrow
are nothing more than all those other hues of green that
like a cow the soul ruminates and savors.

—translated from the Portuguese by Alexis Levitin and Ricardo Vasconcelos

Ashley Kunsa

The New Manifest Destiny

I can't talk about the west without talking about betrayal,
about a place I had to come, but didn't belong,

and knew it. Believing I had spent all my years
in grief's anteroom, I packed my car with what doesn't make

a life but describes it—the bear carried from childhood,
a few dozen photographs, the same off-key smile

that passed unloved from generation to generation,
across an ocean, over a river, back again—and journeyed

alone, battling my mother in the full regalia of
    her misunderstanding.
Or, refusal to understand entwined like a lover with
    the certainty

of her convictions. But the place I arrived was
    more question
than answer, the way a graveyard, in the right light, might be

imagined a garden: the lilies and larkspur in rows,
rising from what was to what becomes. A mistake

anyone could make, and many do, and not without
knowing better. Still, there were times I was certain

apologies must sleep in this soil, though to find them
you'd have to claw past the bones of arrows and horses,

learn to unlace roots that had spent a lifetime taking hold.
You'd have to remember what you had so cultivated

forgetting. Tonight, Mother, at the edge of this familiar
wilderness, you can no more understand me than I can

explain myself. Tonight I'm wandering farther
from home than I've dared before when I ask

about the limits of love and the limits love places
on the places our hearts can beat. I'm writing to you

when I wonder about promises—the ones we make
and the ones that make us—and what takes a girl

thirty-five years to dig out from her own heart like coal
from the rotted belly of a once-green hillside, her hands

so black she mistakes them for night—no, for guilt. For
something she thought she drove away from years ago.

Kristene Kaye Brown

A Walk, A Remembrance

Some days I get nothing right.
                    Some days the winds shift

and darkness enters the body,
but when the ankle-high grasses at last unwind,

and we finish our long walk
with the sound of our conversation receding

into the spiral of everything unsaid,
there is a moment when we know

that all the time we've spent together
or apart   will remain the same

and there will be no turning back from the endings
      that ended nothing.

The flute of a chimney opens as the smell of wood
without water

fills the long waste of a Sunday sky.
          An orchestra of bright things

stirring in dark trees.
Yawning chaos of crickets. Winged oak seeds

sailing
on warm air. This is how I want to remember us—

suspended beneath a sun
that burns the dew into a disappearance of white flames.

Birds pinnacled in mid-flight.
This is what it is.

The turning maples curling back into the red
          of themselves.

The starlings finding their way home.
The string that connects you to me and me to you

breaking as the substance of our past
leans into our absence

and the colors of the sky become nothing more
than forgotten light.

Hannah Dow

Love Poem with Iron and Stone

> *"What shall I say? Men are like air to me, you can't live without them. Every now and then I breathe good fresh air, you know."*
>
> —Katie Sandwina

Maybe love, after all, is not
what lifts a man high above
your shoulders or spins him
like a rifle in a drill-sergeant's
routine. Not what bends him willingly
as iron in your hands, the fire
you give him so hot it leaves you
cold as the stone they say
you're made of. Not, when it's over,
how you pull him into the arc of your body,
almost enough to make him disappear.

You've been thinking that love is a way
of forgetting. Bending a shape into

an unfamiliar shape. Breaking the links
of a chain. That maybe love is the bridge
you make of yourself when they say
love is stronger than anything, because you know
that you and you alone can endure
the weight of an army crossing the truss
that is your body without your heart,
that lonely muscle, giving way.

After Catie Rosemurgy

Hannah Dow

Mother Language

Crystal Bridges Museum of Art

At the outdoor light and sound installation,
shimmering blue bulbs foxtrot to the language
of trees. To some, I suspect this resembles art
less than an expensive Christmas installation:
the kind you drive by in your car and set the radio to,
with an electricity bill that would make

my mother convulse. My mother, who sets
the thermostat between sixty and sixty-three degrees
inside the cocoon of her New England winters,
whose hands purple, crack, and crust from cold,

and because cold hastens temper and forgiveness,
it's never long before we fight
and make up, her fingers warming the spaces
between my own, a throb of heartbeats in my palm.
This way I've memorized her knuckles,
grooved like antique knobs, thumb-nail
nacreous from an incident with the car door,
and callouses: language of the body's

tenderness. I shoot a wordless video of the lights
to send to her, uncertain what she'll see in it.
Watching it later, I notice my finger has eclipsed
the camera's eye. That, and the faint
blue pulsing in the background.

Gary Fincke

Hands: A Memoir

Modeling Hands
My great uncle, for decades, was a hand model. His right hand alone or both of them together displayed in magazines and newspapers. He always took such good care of his hands, my mother said more than once. According to my father, my great-uncle's hands looked as if they had never done a day's work. Like they had never touched anything but themselves.

Working Hands
Five nights a week, my father's hands were white with flour they were dusted with to ease the handling of one-pound sections of bread dough and for rolling smaller bits of dough into spheres. Hundreds of times each night, with both hands, he shaped that dough into sandwich buns and Parkerhouse rolls.

Crossed Hands
I was five when one of my uncles died from throat cancer. He was thirty-one, a heavy smoker who consumed three packs a day. He was laid out for viewing in a coffin in the living room of my grandfather's house. His hands were folded one over

the other just below where his suitcoat was buttoned. Like he was waiting for something.

Changed Hands

During a break in the viewing hours for all of the close relatives to eat lunch in the kitchen, I had to pass through the living room to reach the stairs that led up to the bathroom. With nobody else around, my uncle looked different. Like the body wasn't his. I touched his hands. They felt like the hands on my sister's dolls. My first secret. One I kept.

Praying Hands

Two years before I entered first grade, I started attending Sunday School. The teacher showed us how to make a tepee with our hands when we prayed. Only our fingertips touching. To encourage us, she taught us to flip our hands and thrust our right-hand fingers up between those on our left hands while we chanted a song that went "Here is the church/There is the steeple/Open the door/And see all the people."

Modeling Hands

"You can't have any broken fingers, no scarring, no moles and no marks," my mother said when she mentioned my great-uncle's hand modeling. "And the fingernails have to be perfect. He's always kept them nice even after he stopped modeling." My father said, "If he let his nails grow longer, his hands would look like a woman's."

Praying Hands

When I was in second grade, my mother said, "You're a big boy now. That's enough of the steeple song. Just press one hand against the other just below your chin when you pray."

Working Hands

Week after week, when I was twelve, "He's Got the Whole World in his Hands" was the Number One song on the radio. The singer sounded as young as I was. The song never identified who "He" was, but even a five-year-old would know it was God.

Both Hands

Boys had to climb hand over hand up thick ropes in seventh grade gym class. Half way to the ceiling, exhausted and struggling, barely inching up, I grew terrified I would fall. "Whatever you do, don't slide down," the gym teacher said, but that's exactly what I did. My hands were fierce with heat. "What did I say? Get that taken care of," the teacher said. Blood seeped from where the skin had broken. "Take a shower first," he added. "That's an order."

Working Hands

That same year, in history class, during our six days with myths, Atlas held all of us in place, using his legs and back. His hands helped to balance the planet, but he looked unhappy in his labor, like a hard-working man underappreciated by his boss.

Changed Hands

After our Boy Scout meeting, David Dorner grabbed me by the arm and held up a section of pipe. “Pretty cool, huh?” he said. I stared at the pipe. It reminded me of sinks and toilets, but I didn’t say anything. “If you want to blow something up, all you have to do is light the fuse and boom!” I nodded, but didn’t act excited. Dorner went to a different school. He was nobody I had to impress. A few days later, I heard that when he lit the fuse, the pipe blew up in his hand. I wondered what his screaming sounded like. My father said Dorner had lost three fingers. He never came back to Boy Scouts.

Both Hands

My father’s cousin had a son who was two years younger than me. Once, when we were playing together, he said he was so tired he had to sit down on the ground. He held his hands against the sides of his head, his mouth falling open like the man in the poster the art teacher had shown us. Like he was screaming to himself.

Crossed Hands

When my Sunday School class was mostly thirteen-years-old, we were confirmed on Palm Sunday. Before that ceremony, we learned the perfect position to receive the body of Christ, kneeling to lay our open left hand upon the right. We were supplicants and learned the proper way to reach for wine, letting the blood of Christ be passed down to our half-raised hands from the minister’s tray of tiny cups. Communion was like pity on the part of God, his charity approaching us with a patronizing snack. A man from the congregation followed the minister with an empty tray so we could return those cups.

Modeling Hands
My mother said, "Your great-uncle wore gloves when working around the house and tried to avoid intense cold or heat." When I asked what a hand model was needed for, she said, "To sell watches and sport coats and cuff links and ties."

Working Hands
That year, I started to work in the bakery for a few hours on Friday nights. When I helped with rolling sandwich bun dough, I could only make spheres with my right hand. "Just make circles," my father said, but none of the pieces of dough cupped in my left hand turned into anything but small white turds.

Both Hands
My second cousin, the boy who held his head, had leukemia. After he died, my father told me I was to be a pall bearer. The job was more than lifting the coffin with both hands. "You have to use just one hand to help carry," my father said. I made sure to stand on the side where I could use my right hand to grip a handle. Two of my cousins were older. Another was a man with small children. They took most of the weight of the coffin while I held on and tried not to trip and fall.

Working Hands
"Wash hands after using" was taped above the rust-stained sink beside the terrible bakery basement toilet. Bacteria closed bakeries. They hid inside the near future like failure.

Modeling Hands
My mother had a small scrapbook of clipped ads that featured my great-uncle's hands. Here, she said, are his, and there, too. It was like taking an IQ test. Which of these are identical? Which one of those doesn't belong?

Both Hands
The pall bearers rode to the cemetery in a limousine. My left hand was as soft and unmarked as ever, but a white groove slashed across my right hand. As we rode, the groove darkened to red. When I looked while we stood by the grave, the mark had vanished. Silence shouldered in among us on the way back to the funeral home. No one talked about the inconceivable or any of the other in- words: incomplete, incurable, inconsolable, incensed. As if I'd stolen them from my aunt's black handbag, I kept those words to myself, afraid to spend them.

Crossed Hands
A new minister decided that the wafers were to be laid directly on our tongues. Our hands, unoccupied, gripped the railing as we knelt or were clasped for a pose of piety while we waited for wine to sip from the common cup wiped dry after each upraised mouth had altered it. All of us were infants at the rail, our hands used only for balance as we

rose, steadying ourselves, returning to the hardwood pews, Christian families with histories, ready to sing the recessional hymn, verses releasing us into weather that waited outside, regardless of communion and prayer, fathers retrieving their cars like valets, their wives and children waiting in the doorways like the wealthy.

Working Hands
Years before, bare-handed, a man who worked for my father had pulled a pan of sandwich buns from the oven without burning himself. My father, some Fridays, would tell that story whenever miracles were mentioned. As if we needed faith, as if that man never again forgot his insulated gloves.

Both Hands
Before sleep, my hands loved the brief pleasure they made, my body remembering the beautiful parts of girls from my invisible place in their lives.

Praying Hands
Except for pretending in church, I gave up praying. In order to be convincing when I lip-synched the familiar prayers, I gripped my hands together in front of my chest.

Modeling Hands
My mother said that moisturizing was important to my great-uncle. "He used to moisturize a dozen times a day," she said. "About once an hour."

Working Hands
My mother worked in the bakery for twelve hours every Saturday. Just before closing, she scrubbed pans while steam spread around her. Her hands, when she finished, were always red.

Both Hands
"What small hands," a girl told me, "for someone your size," and I pulled them away from where she had been running her fingers over my palms, tracing what she called my life lines. I wondered if she knew what that assessment meant. Every boy in the high school did.

Praying Hands
My mother, for years, had a set of dish towels embroidered with praying hands, the palms pressed together in a way that was unmistakable.

Both Hands
Half of the basketball team could palm the ball with either hand. I didn't even try. I dribbled away when they swung an arm around, the ball firmly in one hand.

The Huns of Time
There's no escaping the Huns of time, my great-aunt said, or seemed to, her teeth badly fitted. The Huns of time, she said, are never satisfied, no reasoning with them, intending, I thought, to make me see the ways the Huns could invade me. Some afternoons, when I was doing nothing but slouching in front of our small television, I thought I could hear the

Huns of time muttering among themselves outside. Some evenings, when the Huns slipped inside, I could tell they'd quit school, that they moved a lot because they couldn't hold jobs. Always, though, the Huns were having fun, more of it, at least, than parents like mine who were punctual as dawn. The Huns of time laughed a lot. They swallowed beer and wine in gulps. Wasn't there always plenty of time? And didn't it return the next day? No wonder the Huns looked so happy. Their families were sure to join them, coming from over the horizon where they pillaged like darkness or light.

Both Hands
I was never able to master using my left hand in basketball, not for dribbling, not even for an uncontested layup.

Changed Hand
During my senior year, there was a student teacher who had a prosthetic hand. Although I never saw him use it, the hand seemed perfectly formed, something like a mannequin's hand, only soft and pliable.

Working Hands
Once I had a driver's license, I began to work in the bakery on Friday nights from ten o'clock to five-thirty. My father left the front door open until after the bars closed at two a.m. Occasionally I waited on men who believed, leaving the two nearby bars, they needed cupcakes or cookies or small pies. Afterwards, before returning to my regular work, I had to go downstairs to the sink and scrub my hands after handling the small bills and change I had to touch.

Changed Hands
I read about a woman born with three fingers who experienced, after amputation, a phantom hand with five fingers. As if those bones had needed years of weather to expose them, an old crime revealed from a life lived long before this one.

Working Hands
Though rare, there were nights when a woman, drunk, would lean across the glass counter, a loose blouse falling open as if she was inviting my hands. My trip downstairs would include private pleasure before I scalded my hands before finishing the work I owed my father. Afterward, I slept until noon, waking to lunch without washing, holding a thick, pressed meat sandwich, stuffing it down my throat because now I wasn't working for anybody but myself.

Both Hands
When, at last, a girl touched my body with her hands, I inhaled so sharply I sounded like someone I didn't know.

Changed Hands
Although rare, there have been cases of men and women who bite off fingers from their own hands. Often, they beg to be restrained. If left alone, they disfigure themselves.

Both Hands
After working in the bakery for five years, I still could not roll sandwich bun dough into spheres with my left hand.

Praying Hands

When my wife learned she was pregnant with our first child, I went with her to the nearest gynecologist. Both of us stared at the half dozen posters of praying hands framed and hung on the waiting room walls. There were pamphlets that explained that the doctor would always save the baby rather than the mother if a choice had to be made in the delivery room. The doctor, when we met him, confirmed that. "My faith guides that decision," he said. That same afternoon we sought out a different doctor.

Working Hands

I learned to type with more than two fingers. My hands sped over the keys except for my little fingers, which refused to work. A magazine article declared the world smaller, the globe shriveling from the cold of technology until it fit in the soft palms of the wealthy. By then I thought that the world wasn't as simple as that. It was more complicated, something worse.

Modeling Hands

My great-uncle lived forty years beyond when he hand-modeled. A few months before he died, he visited with my parents the same evening my wife and our first child were there. His hands were mottled and liver spotted, but they looked to be nearly wrinkle-free. When we shook hands before he left, his hands were soft, even delicate despite his age. As if he had never ceased caressing them with lotions and creams.

Both Hands

My daughter, an artist, teaches anatomy to small children, beginning, each year, with the hands. Her daughter, at six, drew my hands like a camera. At eight, she sketched my face so perfectly I feared that my secrets could be revealed through her accomplished hands.

Brian Phillip Whalen

Tip of The Tongue (Lethologica)

There is a word, I'm certain,
          for sunsets in the eastern sky
or for northern dusk

when North is far, far
          away.
I'm in Alabama

on a Tuesday
          brewing tea from a tin
from Albany, New York,

where you are—
          or were,
the last we spoke.

It was summer then,
          a gentle rain;
the sun had set. We hugged,

miscalculating:
        arm goes where—?
Tonight, in the deep south, in winter,

your name
        (*trochaic*) in my mouth
is as soft

as first I spoke it—speaking *you*
        into my world,
four short years

before *farewell,*
        farewell.
The tea I drink this evening

is *oolong,* and the sky
        has turned, in the time it took
to write this,

a deep, unnamable
        blue. Any minute now
another darkness

will erase this twilight—
        and the word, it must be,
is *longing.*

Lance Larson

Last Night I Touched a Great Horned Owl

Or thought I did. Not a god of the sky after all,
but a rooster roosting. Shadows confused me,
that rooster's glorious comb. Who cares?
At midnight, in an alley, when you reach out
your hand, even chicken feathers feel ancient
and archetypal and true. Can roosters groan
in their rooster sleep? This one did and I groaned
with it. Hell, maybe the entire Earth groans
and we just have to learn how to listen. Even
peripatetic St. Paul reminds us we know not
what to pray for but the spirit itself "maketh
intercession for us with groanings that cannot
be uttered." I groaned all the way home,
groans steeped in moonlight and wonder.
Did gravel in the alley groan with me,
branches tossing in the wind? I think so.
Now it's morning, and the sun blooms
everywhere, and I'm walking to the mailbox:
maybe Apollo was the kind of driver
who scared groans out of his wandering steeds.
And maybe Icarus was an ascending groan

waiting to melt? Once, in Pablo Neruda's
house in Valparaíso, I heard the Atlantic
groan. He designed the house to resemble
a schooner, five rickety stories hugging a hill.
When I closed my eyes, I heard giant squids
and mermaids groan, nautical sadness
wafting in from the bay. I was standing
in the breeze, as if in a crow's nest.
Do groans that tall and salty count as vision?
Now I'm carrying the mail back inside.
I sit down in the living room and put up
my feet, and the coffee table holds forth,
a sawhorse of splintery groans. Can an ordinary
rock groan? Some rocks we crush, some we crack
open for purple palaces inside, some we skip
across flat water. Other rocks, like this piece
of Halite on the table, are pure crystals. I taste it
when I'm nervous or sad, each salty lick a groan.
A birthday gift my geologist dad brought back
from Mexico fifty years ago. What I wanted
back then was an iguana. Or thought I wanted.
If I lick this chunk of salt 10,000 times,
it will disappear but maybe he'll return.
Dear Father, dear Midnight Owl, dear Iguana,
dear Sky, dear Whoever wherever
you are, I can almost taste you, my tongue
groaning for a little salt, and then a little more.

Lance Larsen

Two Mornings After the Capitol Insurrection, We Go Birding

Rank amateurs, my wife and I, but we have binocs,
a smart phone, a wetlands map, and dozens of trails
to traipse. Who could have guessed we were just nine miles
east of the Las Vegas Strip? And in twenty minutes
we've crossed off five birds. Coot, mallard, pintail,
roadrunner, and sparrow. Then I tender a little
harshness (It's a song sparrow, look at its head)
and she tenders back (What are you smoking?
try lark sparrow), and for the sake of marital bliss,
we split up, her to the swamp where she can nap,
and me to the observation bridge where I can pace.
And the morning is sad rapture, and the sky sizzles blue,
and the birds of east Las Vegas are getting along
swimmingly with the breeze and sun and algae
and photosynthesis and hoofy tourists like me.
If there's a voice to follow here, it's the voice
of nature, part St. Francis of Assisi, part Holy Ghost.
And there's a fattish dad and his bellowing kid,
who won't sit in his mostly collapsed collapsible

stroller with a gimpy wheel. And a bicyclist racing
his own testosterone. And a golden retriever
sniffing every millimeter of my mopiness. And now
the screamer is rolling on the ground and greeting
the avian world with nonstop drool and snot.
And Mr. Dad, crouched like a gargoyle, misses
the morning's one revelation—a great white egret
rising from the reeds like a god on fire, like a whispery
displacement of gravity, who lifts and banks away,
rearranging the sky. That's right, misses his one shot
to trade rancor for patience, flesh for light.
As for me, I saw the egret without my beloved,
which is like seeing nothing at all. So I return my gaze
to the armada of coots and watch the dad sideways
to check what comes next. Problem Solving 101:
if two things are bugging the hell out of you, rid
yourself of one. Which the dad promptly does,
good and swift dad, solutions dad, by picking up
the stroller that won't stroll and winging it
from the bridge. It's a sublime sight, that umbrella
gizmo going end over end, light pink, light pink,
a broken pterodactyl, and when it hits, coots
and mallards scatter, and it slowly sinks, as if into
a bubbling tarpit. And I want to hide this maniac dad
from the warden (are there wardens here?) and I want
to shake his expressive Neanderthal right hand.
Instead I concentrate on the closest of coots, white
beak, black body, bob bob bob, dive, where will you
come up for air this time, Mr. Magician? And for
this wounded father there's nothing left to do but pick

up his enemy, which is also his kin, and move through space and time, hugging this screamer to his chest.

Lance Larsen

I Ask Advice of Caliban

What a drippy, stoopy, gorgeous creature, oozing
across the stage like a melted man, then twenty
minutes later, mostly tidied up, on the same train
as me hurtling east towards Camden Town.
He had a diet Coke in his hand, smears of makeup
on his neck. Of course I plied him with questions.
Skip the West End, he said, *skip the London Eye,*
skip Madame Tussauds, but catch every play playing
at the Arcola. And the National ain't bad. Check out
the Handel & Hendrix Museum in Mayfair, he said—
now that's a bang-up marriage. He wasn't scuttling
like a crab now or slurping raw eggs or biting air
around Miranda's face. I liked him, this Caliban
and not Caliban, but trust him? *Mud larking*
is a lark, he said, *especially out by Kew, and there's good*
Ethiopian to be had in Finsbury Park. Me? he said.
I always wanted to be Ariel, to flit and tease like that,
vengeful wasp, but I'm too meaty. He was against
Brexit but for immortality, as in actors writing
their own plays. Against the hordes at Stonehenge
but all in for Druids. *Try Aylesbury instead,*

where you can walk around and rub the ruins and take
a selfie with a sheep. By now, our train was tunneling
through rain and mist, a lozenge in the throat
of who knew what? And the Thames was a thought
experiment in tides, and London was trying
to turn us all into fog. But we were still
Calibans, with our meaty breath and rusted chains.
Swim, he said, *whether at Brighton or the Serpentine*
or at Hampstead Heath, I don't care where, just swim,
that's the real King's English, throw yourself into the cold
waters with Grendel and practice how not to bloody drown.

Rob Roensch

Popsicle Stick Cathedral

The county was so desperate for teachers they didn't fire me, but instead insisted I admit I had a problem and stop drinking, which I mostly did. In the fall, the school they sent me to was further out: NO TRESPASSING signs posted on barbed wired fences enclosing empty fields, a daycare called Precious Angels in an old Pizza Hut.

In my new classroom there was a jumble of scarred folding tables, paint-spattered stools clustered around each one. I could have arranged them more sensibly; I did not.

In the last class of the first day there was one boy who no one would sit with. He was ordinary looking: freckles, short hair, sneakers and shorts and T-shirt like everyone else (though it would become clear after several weeks that he, alone of the boys, never wore a shirt with Thunder or Sooner logos, never any words in jagged energy-drink font). The second day I ordered half of a packed-full table to move over to his. There was no grumbling, but only blank compliance, as if I was an adult, a woman to be respected. The day after that he was again alone.

The teachers at the school either have been there forever or they'll never belong. There are so many my-mothers. So many giant cheerful toddlers. Then there is the eighth-grade math teacher who looks like death and used to work on supersonic aircraft. The PE teacher who indoors is wide-eyed, a deer stuck in a mall. Me.

Once upon a time I was going to move to New York. My portfolio was the end result of months of being annoyed by what other people put on the radio in an alternately mossy-or-bleachy smelling corner of a studio used also as storage for sculpture courses: nests of twisted wire and melting mannequin collisions. I sat atop a stool with uneven legs that ticked back and forth to work; I could have switched stools, but I did not. Working from photographs of strangers, I produced thirty-six open-hand-sized studies of parts of open eyes. Up on the wall for critique it looked like nothing, like a bunch of tacked-up postcards.

For the color wheel assignment (a requirement noted on page 2 of my extremely lightly used curriculum binder), the lonely boy painted a haunted blue and orange bird perched on top of a long low brick building that I saw right away was an uncannily accurate representation of the school we were inside of.

I decided to run the unit on clay pinch-pot "sculptures" (a unit I knew from experience that could be messy but would at least keep them occupied) but I discovered that I had of course not thought to put in the order for the clay ahead of time. So, the supply closet: along with reams of crummy construction paper and tubs of crayons and jugs of paint, was a shelf full of staplers and chalk, quarter-full bottles of white squirt glue, giant cans of ketchup for some reason, and promising looking taped-up boxes that turned out to be full of popsicle sticks and toothpicks. I asked the kids what they wanted to make and they looked up at me like I was supposed to know.

Some mornings on the drive out to school there are millions of birds on the power lines; I noticed them more once the leaves started falling; the wind sometimes was a giant vacuum sucking them all up into towering swirls. I wouldn't say I'm lost. What I would say is that I have always had a sense that there is something I have to do but I don't know what it is.

Out of bored desperation to plan the next unit, I spent a not terrible evening on popsicle stick Youtube. The next day, before I introduced the architecture assignment, I placed piles of toothpicks and popsicle sticks on all the tables, along with, for each table, one tub of rubber cement, one new squeeze bottle of white glue, a roll of scotch tape.

The third day of popsicle stick architecture, the students came into class and went immediately to the drying racks to bring out their projects without my having to order them. We quickly discovered that white glue often failed. Under the closet ketchup tins, a box of never-opened masking tape, which you could draw or paint on better than scotch tape. The next day, for each project I brought in a photograph of a relevant building for inspiration—the Coliseum, a New England farmhouse, Notre Dame of Laon--that I printed out on my never-used photo-printer, a gift from my parents. We discussed the Golden Ratio, the worth of windows.

The lonely boy worked alone, standing up. He'd brought in a set of fine-tipped color markers of his own that he used to saturate individual toothpicks that he then laid out in rows before joining them into walls, corners, arches.

There were stacks of small cheap paper cups next to the sink. One day one of the stacks was on the lonely boy's table. It turns out the cups could easily be disassembled into useful pieces: the stiff rim could be cut out and pulled straight, the bottoms could be cut into translucent white circles, the body of the cup could be unpeeled and cut into any useful shape. It was stiffer than paper, but waxy enough to be easily manipulated. Soon everyone wanted cups. I found several bags of them jammed behind a tub of snow-melt salt in the corner of the supply closet. The half-done architectural models grew new elements: flags, turrets, weathervanes, window shades.

Alone in my room after school one day, I set out all of the popsicle stick architecture projects. Walking among them was oddly peaceful, like driving into the city at dawn. There were a couple OSU and OU stadiums, including one guarded by a team of army guys painted maroon. An almost Eiffel tower half rainbow-colored. A castle with a functioning drawbridge and a Lego queen.

The lonely boy had constructed a cathedral: spires, a great central steeple. He'd used what looked at first like too much blue but then, upon further attention, was not. There was no door in.

The next morning when the kids came into the classroom, I had them line up against the sink counter and wait. I'd stacked the stools in a corner and pulled all the tables to right angles and spaced them evenly and then arranged the models on top. I talked about how to experience art, which is also how to live, I once knew. I talked about how to take your time, about how to see the work from the perspective of its creator, about how paying careful attention to the world was a kind of prayer. Then I invited them to look.

Most kids at least tried to follow directions, leaned in closely, making hilarious imitations of serious faces, making serious faces, looking.

I was not surprised to find that the class, minus some logo-shirted boys in the far corner doing something with something in their pockets, soon clustered around the lonely boy's cathedral.

"How can anybody even do that?" said a normal girl to no one, even though the lonely boy stood among them.

A reply began to assemble itself in my mind, about how the focused expression of a unique imagination is evidence of the inherent value of each individual soul when in the same moment the lonely boy leaned forward and brought the double hammer of his fists down on the popsicle stick cathedral. It didn't shatter, but smushed inward, somehow flesh-like. He raised his fists to repeat the act and I stepped forward and grabbed one and held it up and grabbed his other shoulder to keep him still and he grunt-whined, through his nose, and did not look at me. He was not strong.

The other kids stayed where they were, as if this was not unexpected.

"You're not supposed to put hands on anyone," said a normal girl to me, not like a tattletale, but blankly, like a bank teller. I looked in her face. It was set; she knew how things worked. At first I wasn't going to ever let go, but then I did, and the lonely boy dashed off, into the hall.

The next day he was again at his table, alone. I assigned two other kids, nice kids, to sit at his table. I didn't let them abandon him.

Here, the sky is infinitely far away and also everywhere. In the winter the early morning skies are baby blues and comic-book bright pinks and translucent oranges with clouds like cotton balls pulled apart and smeared on glass. Outside my apartment the landscape is flat and in one distance suburban and repetitive and in the other bare, scraggled and prickly, like someone combed all the green and life up and out. But I feel very alive, and I am painting again. It's not that the work I am creating is perfect, or complete, but my relationship to it has changed. Sometimes I imagine taking my work in my hands and tearing it and crushing it, destroying it like the lonely boy destroyed the popsicle stick cathedral.

Frank Paino

Pieta: Father Mychal Judge

after the iconic photo of the
priest's body being carried out of
the World Trade Center's North
Tower on 9/11

Worse than fire fed by kerosene,
than towers turned to their own black vanishing,
worse than his already waxen hand,
its elegant fingers that seem poised for benediction,
is the square of flesh that must not have seen the sun
all that long summer, a glimpse of slender tibia
over which he'd pulled his plain cotton sock
when the morning was still ordinary,
still decipherable as a painted allegory
where ash-grey stands for a terrible quietude,
as in marble made to bear an unbearable grief—
or the way men can emerge from a shroud of steel
and cinder carrying the slack weight of one fallen.
As if death is a burden they can help him carry.

Ann Keniston

Self-Portrait as my First Memory

That grief's a turning place
                    or choice

          occurs to me
sometimes. Sometimes a neutral

memory grows bright
          with it. Sometimes it feels

                    as light

as balloons near the ceiling of
          an indoor

                    space. I recall a ramp
in pastel hues, light
          falling through a glass-walled

                    room like a movie
clip spliced-in,

just three or four seconds
I've turned into
a gate and neutral

shield. There were

stuffed bears for children who
were sick. But where's

the turn, the place
I can't turn back from or fall

more deeply in? It turns

in me, my innards
curved around
its curves, an emptiness

that lifts
like helium or

held breath
or air puffed
around a pebble in a bag until

it almost floats, which
is also the grief.

Ken Meisel

Poem with Anguish in It

Everything I'm about to say might have happened,

& if it's true
I'd like to tell you the night never forgets
what it gives away.

& if there was a woman, she committed herself
to a mystery,

& if she walked, wrapped by a shawl into trees,
it might have been because of heartache

or a song she was following.
& if I saw her first, exiting a Super 8 motel
where she strolled self-silent & alone,

I might have even figured to myself she *was* alone,
even if she wasn't.

& things can go wrong, & we enter at various points,

& secrets are what we keep, when we have no one
to confess to,
& if that is true, she glided past a dive bar
where the patrons were howling & gambling

& there might have been a man in there
familiar to her, maybe her ex-husband, or her father,

or maybe just her next door neighbor—
a fellow she'd smoke with—

& sometimes belief is what we ask
another to undress from us

& maybe one night stands are just two strangers,
undressing beliefs from each other

so they can feel free enough to care again,

& I never had a one-night stand
that took away my anguish—

even though a few willing partners tried,
& so did I—

but the anguish is just a homesickness
without a door to relieve it. So we give into it,
& it makes us stronger, wiser somehow.

& maybe the morning is for regret,
& the night is how we make it,

but this woman kept walking out of town

until she was a mushroom shape.
& when she entered the trees

I saw her un-cape her shawl & let it drop
like a burden

& she started running—
not away from something but *to* something—

& maybe release
is what all the sadness is truly asking of us

& I couldn't see or hear her

but there was a light, & I think it was over
a river

where a big water tower rose up,
& this is where I'm making the rest up

because all I see is her, climbing the tower

where she sees her brother, way up there,
readying himself to jump
to where the hard concrete waits

for his body to hit it, like a meteor.

I guess this poem is about her younger brother.

& so here's the part I tell her:

when someone leaves us, we follow them
until they tell us *not* to, & he hasn't yet,

he hasn't told her, *Don't you dare come for me.*
I think he's still waiting for her, he's looking for her.

& here's the awful truth—she has to say *Please don't do it*
to him
because he's going to jump anyway. He's a goner,

& he needs her to witness it—
so he's remembered by her, in his last act.

And sometimes people feel so powerless, so alone
that they create a stage-setting for one last act.

& sadness is just a ball of anguish we release
from ourselves in order to know where we begin or end—

especially when someone we love stages a last act—

so that we can enter the human riddle of love again,
& be stronger for it. Somehow, some way, again.

& maybe I'm supposed to trail her,

& shake her a bit & hold her,
because he tells me to,
so she has someone there beside her.
Someone to tell someone else—like you—
about this ordeal she's gone through.

About all the anguish inside it.
& maybe that's what this poem's about.

Kevin Clark

Dexter's Reed

"I'm a Fool to Want You"
—Dexter Gordon

Staring at the ceiling tonight is staring down
without falling
in. A floating above the widening aperture
as Dexter's reed
rasps along the precipice
of longing. There's no bottom

to the pitch of sadness vocalizing this air. Songs
ago, the end
of visiting hours dissolved my wife's hand
like prophecy.
In the beginning, who ever truly believes
first touch lasts

as love? So young on meeting, I hadn't trusted
the future. Her savvy laugh
still mocks
that old worry. Earbuds wired past 2AM, I can't hear

the heart
monitors beeping through the halls, only

the urgent squeaking work shoes of the night nurse
ever *en route* to check
on me. I turn my back to the chiaroscuro
shock
of the blazing door, aggrieved
to have broken

from the big man's swoon. Yesterday they said maybe
it's no embolism after all.
Could be nothing
more than a trapezius pull, but the machines
can't be sure, leaving me
suspended with Dexter. The endless bottom

is an endless blues-sweet roil, love unfurled
into an upswell
of grief,
as if the perfectly worn reed foreshadows
exhalation's last tone. A question
beyond answer. Five miles off, my wife's alarm

will chime its get-to-work song. I picture her
morning's ritual reach
across the bed into
absence. Dexter endures—now the short pause
of an easy breath

outside the quotidian slap-dash of a clock's goings-
and-gones. Unlike his lover,
my wife's not
gone. But doesn't the horn's last decrescendo predict
all parting?
I'm the reed shred into silence.

Kevin Clark

Reading Larry Levis at Dusk in November

1.
Maybe it's true, as Henry Miller said, that the greats
Are all cracked with certitude—

Take Larry's boy in the video arcade, a blade
Buried in his torn jeans, his bleeding knees

Mashing the machine as if it were school,
A sullen kiss-off to death. Take

That stunned soldier, his arms stretched like welcome
Over the trees of Shiloh…

In and of themselves, okay, both are brute rendering.
But don't we want to make something better of it all?

Or is that urge called just-getting-by?
Pedaling home past the university meat plant yesterday

I looked up across the road to see Cuesta Grade turned out
In windy grace, as if the drought-dull greens

Had lit from within, irradiated by the setting sun—
A planned spectacle, a thing

Blissed with purpose.

Like Larry, there was a time I'd see such beauty
As testament

To all that's missing in this world. The utter null
Of the verdant. I love the man's poems,

Despite his great agonizing loss of faith
In any magic, any mystery in the universe. The song

Inborn in nearly every line he wrote is testament
To just that: a hidden undecodable

Absence. Don't you want to float

For a while on his soft thermal? Sure,
I could be fooling myself lately. Have I twinged

The absolute into a redeeming question? I don't know,
But I keep thinking,

What if it's true—
That a photon dancing miles away from its twin

Follows its lead in perfect synch?
Are we then halfway to saved by the inexplicable?

2.
—Or am I pressing my own ever-echoing *what-ifs*
Too far beneath the widening spell of Larry's leaves,

The ones spread out on the Carpathian Frontier
In October of 1968 where he drove

Alone while his appendix worsened,

Comforted briefly as the leaves swept across the road
And settled like a prismatic carpet spooled out

In pain-killing beauty just for him? That next month
I flew north to Jersey from college, skeletal

From running cross-country, the first leaves of crape myrtle
And Chicasaw plum spotting the clay paths

Of north Florida. It was my time to deny god

Like the pain rising each day as micro-tears turned
The stems of my legs stronger. Truth is, I'd tired

Over the tropical hillocks, sick of my breath cadenced
Across the humid miles, sick

Of the incessantly voiceless god

I'd grown up with. Tonight, as Venus rises in my window,
I want to imagine the photons of its light

Flickering upon these pages like a signal
At the very moment Larry looks back to Mr. Hirata,

His family's portrait photographer who would die
Behind the gates of Manzanar. Maybe

That's it: Every line Larry breathed infused the air
With the kind of threnody

Intent on bringing back the dead.

Before my family choralled into grace, before
My mother stood me at the table's head in place

Of my father to carve the bird, I stole out to
    the front drive
With a patio chair in the chill, surely

Crosscut by memory streams of my father's voice

Revivified in the air despite his young death
    five years earlier.
And so I sat to study the dark tips

Of the leafless oaks of New Jersey as they chiaroscuro
the last lit blues of evening.

3.
Okay. Maybe I misfigured Larry's project.
I'm coming to think his lyric didn't betray

An honest disbelief in god. Yes, his doubt was inviolable.
But wasn't he writing *after* Mr. Hirata? After

The boy in the arcade whose vacant gut was filling
With the clotted bile of his own resentment. After

The dead man whose spread arms mocked the ground
Below the torn trees of Shiloh? Even

After that bay cowhorse from Piedra? He loved

All of them, caught as they were in the ruthless
Unstoppable declination that may stab you

In the side without warning, that would kill him at 48,
That would kill my father before his time—

As so many neighbors were compelled to tell me at fourteen
As they drank hard in the old manner of Catholic wakes—

Though even then I'd never believed there's such a thing
As owning rights to time. I know

Larry would never grant the import of photons

Precisely entangled in their implausible dance, but
I *do* believe

That in the immeasurably far off region of space
Within us, undetectable neutrinos

Pass through, beyond notice of poetry.

—Even as the boy in the arcade lets the cigarette match
Char the tips of his fingers without flinching.

And Mr. Hirata once again says, Please smile now.
And the soldier's arms at Shiloh

Descend at dusk to make whole his body.

—Even as my father's eyes lift from the page I'm holding.
Even as, once more, the book

Closes itself.

Contributors' Notes

Ernesto L. Abeytis has had work in such journals as *Prairie Schooner*, *Fugue*, and *Crab Orchard Review*. **John Bradley**'s most recent book is *Hotel Montparnasse: Letters to Cesar Vallejo*. His poetry has appeared in such journals as *American Poetry Review*, *Caliban*, *Hotel Amerika*, and *Diagram*. He is a poetry editor for *Cider Press Review*. **Kristene Kaye Brown**'s work has appeared in such journals as *New South*, *Nimrod*, *Ploughshares*, and *Salt Hill*. **Terri Brown-Davidson**'s books include *The Carrington Monologues* and *Marie, Marie: Hold On Tight*. Her work has appeared in such journals as *The Virginia Quarterly Review*, *Puerto del Sol*, *Beloit poetry Journal*, and *TriQuarterly*. **Ian Cappelli** is the author of *Suburban Hermeneutics*. His work has appeared in such journals as *The Los Angeles Review*, *The Journal*, and *Atlanta Review*. **Kevin Clark**'s most recent collection is *The Consecrations*. His poetry has appeared in such journals as *The Georgia Review*, *Prairie Schooner*, *Epoch*, *Poetry Northwest*, *The Southern Review*, and *The Denver Quarterly*. **Grant Clauser** is the author of *Muddy Dragon on the Road to Heaven*, winner of the Codhill Press Poetry Award. His poems have appeared in *The American Poetry Review*, *Greensboro Review*, *The Kenyon Review*, and other journals. **Jessica Cuello**'s books include *Liar*, winner of the 2020 Barrow Street Book Prize, and *Yours, Creature.* She has received a number of other awards, including The *New Letters* Poetry Prize and *The New Ohio Review* Poetry Prize. **Michael Czyzniejewski**'s books include *I Will Love You for the Rest of My Life*, *Chicago Stories*, *Elephants in the Bedroom*, and, most recently, *The Amnesiac in the Maze.* **Julie Danho**'s *Those Who Keep Arriving* won the 2018 Gerald Cable Book Award. Her poems have appeared in such journals as *Alaska Quarterly Review*, *Pleiades*, and *New Ohio Review.* **Nathaniel Dolton-Thornton**'s poems have appeared in such journals as *Tin House*, *Gulf Coast*, *Vallum*, *Raritin*, *Sycamore Review*, and *Poetry Salzburg Review.* **Hannah Dow** is the author of *Rosarium.* Her poems have appeared in such journals as *Shenandoah*, *Image*, and *The Southern Review.* **Hollie Dugas**' work has appeared in such journals as *Barrow Street*, *Reed Magazine*, *Crab Creek Review*, *Poet Lore*, *The Louisville Review*, and *Calyx.* **Gary Fincke**'s latest essay collection *The Darkness Call* won the Robert C. Jones Prize. A new collection *The Mayan Syndrome* will be published by Madhat in 2023. The lead essay "After the Three-Moon Era" was reprinted in *Best American Essays 2020.* **Dagne Forrest**'s poetry has appeared in journals in Canada, the US, Australia, and the UK. In 2021 she was one of 15 poets featured in The League of Canadian Poets' annual Poem in Your Pocket campaign, had a poem shortlisted for the UK's Bridport Prize, and won first prize in the Hammond House Publishing International Literary Prize (Poetry). Her creative nonfiction has appeared or is forthcoming in *Paper Dragon* and *Sky Island Journal.* She is an editor with *Painted Bride Quarterly.* **Alice Friman**'s most recent collections are *Blood Weather*,

The View from Saturn, and *Vinculum*. She has had work in *The Pushcart Prize Anthology* and *The Best American Poetry*, and such journals as *Poetry*, *The Georgia Review*, *The Gettysburg Review*, *Poetry East*, and *Ploughshares*. **John Gallaher**'s poem in this issue is from his forthcoming book *My Life in Brutalist Architecture*. **Elton Glaser** is the author of eight collections of poetry, most recently *Translations from the Flesh* and *The Law of Falling Bodies*. **Lola Haskins** is the author of eleven books of poetry and three of prose, and her poetry has appeared in such journals as *The Atlantic*, *the London Review of Books*, *London Magazine*, *The Georgia Review*, and *Prairie Schooner*. **Andrew Hemmert** is the author of *Blessing the Exoskeleton* and *Sawgrass Sky*. His work has appeared in such journals as *Cincinnati Review*, *The Kenyon Review*, *The Southern Review*, and *Prairie Schooner*. **Romana Iorga** is the author of two poetry collections in Romanian. Her work in English has appeared in such journals as *New England Review* and *The Nation*. **Ann Keniston**'s most recent collection is *Somatic*. Her work has appeared in such journals as *The Yale Review* and *The Gettysburg Review*. **Ashley Kunsa**'s work has appeared in such journals as *Bennington Review*, *Blue Mesa Review*, and *Cream City Review*. **Paula J. Lambert**'s most recent collection is *The Ghost of Every Feathered Thing*. She is the editor of Full/Crescent Press. **Lance Larsen**'s most recent collection is *What the Body Knows*. His poems have appeared in *The Southern Review*, *American Poetry Review*, *The Paris Review*, *New England Review*, and *Best American Poetry*. **Alexis Levitin** has published forty-eight books of translation, including Eugenio de Andrade's *Forbidden Words* and Astrid Cabral's *Gazing Through the Water*. He has received two NEA Translation Awards. **Angie Macri** is the author of *Underwater Panther*, winner of the Cowles Poetry Book Prize, and *Fear Nothing of the Future or the Past.* Her work has appeared in *The Carolina Quarterly, Harpur Palate, New England Review,* and *Western Humanities Review.* **Michael Malan** is editor of Cloudbank. His books include *Deep Territory* and *Tarzan's Jungle Plane*, and his work has appeared in such journals as *Cincinnati Review*, *Chicago Quarterly Review*, and *Poetry East.* **Matt Martinson** has work in *Crab Creek Review*, *One Hand Clapping*, and *Coffin Bell Journal.* **Ken Meisel**'s most recent books include *Our Common Souls: New & Selected Poems of Detroit*, *Mortal Lullabies*, and *Studies Inside the Consent of a Distance.* **Luís Miguel Nava**'s *Poesia*, consisting of four completed collections and eighty pages of posthumous publications, came out in 2020, twenty-five years after the young poet's shocking death. Poems drawn from his forthcoming collection in English have been accepted by eighteen magazines, including *Birmingham Poetry Review, Bitter Oleander, Hollins Critic, The Los Angeles Review, Massachusetts Review, Mid-American Review, Poet Lore,* and *Puerto del Sol.* **Frank Paino**'s most recent book is *Obscura* from Orison Books. His poems have appeared in such journals as *North American Review*, *Crab Orchard Review*, and *World Literature Today*, as well as in anthologies such as *The Face of Poetry* and *Beyond Earth's Edge: The Poetry of Spaceflight.* **Aimee Parkison**'s most recent collection is *Suburban Death Project.* Her stories have appeared in such journals as *Five Points*, *The Laurel Review*, *Fictional International*, and *Hotel Amerika.* **Doug Ramspeck** is the author of nine poetry collections, one collection of stories, and a novella. His work has appeared in such journals as *The Southern Review*, *The Kenyon Review*, and *The Georgia Review*. **Rob Roensch**'s most recent book is *The World and the Zoo*. **Nicole Rollender** is the author of *Louder Than Everything You Love*. Her work has appeared in such journals as *Alaska Quarterly Review*, *Ninth Letter*, *Puerto del Sol*, *Salt Hill*, and *West Branch*. **Adam Scheffler**'s *Heartworm* won The Moon City Press Poetry Award. **David Shumate** is the author of *Kimonos in the Closet*, *High Water Mark*, and *The Floating Bridge*. **Stephanie Staab**'s newest chapbook is *Letter-locking*. Her work has appeared in such journals as *Crab Creek Review*, *Chestnut Review*, and *Lunch Ticket*. **Mark Sullivan**'s *Slag* won the Walt McDonald First Book in Poetry Award. His work has appeared in *Cimarron Review*, *Rhino*, *Tar River Poetry*, and *The Best American Essays*. **Andrew R. Touhy** is the author of *Designs for a Magician's Top Hat*, winner of the inaugural Yemassee Fiction Chapbook Prize. His stories appear in *Conjunctions*, *New England Review*, *Alaska Quarterly Review*, *New American Writing*, and other journals. **Ricardo Vasconcelos** is a Professor of Portuguese at San Diego State University. His scholarly work on modern and contemporary Portuguese literature, including Mário de Sá-Carneiro, Fernando Pessoa, and Eça de Queirós, has been published in several countries. **Lauren Watel**'s work has appeared in such journals as *The Paris Review*, *The Nation*, *Tin House*, *The Hudson Review*, *Five Points*, and *The Massachusetts Review*. **Brian Phillip Whalen** is the author of *Semiotic Love*, a collection of stories. His work has appeared in such journals as *The Southern Review*, *Copper Nickel*, *Creative Nonfiction*, and *Lit Hub*.